CULTURE SMART!
CHILE

Caterina Perrone

·K·U·P·E·R·A·R·D·

ISBN 978 1 85733 341 1
This book is also available as an e-book: eISBN 978 1 85733 576 7

British Library Cataloguing in Publication Data
A CIP catalogue entry for this book is available from the
British Library

First published in Great Britain
by Kuperard, an imprint of Bravo Ltd
59 Hutton Grove, London N12 8DS
Tel: +44 (0) 20 8446 2440 Fax: +44 (0) 20 8446 2441
www.culturesmart.co.uk
Inquiries: sales@kuperard.co.uk

Distributed in the United States and Canada
by Random House Distribution Services
1745 Broadway, New York, NY 10019
Tel: +1 (212) 572-2844 Fax: +1 (212) 572-4961
Inquiries: csorders@randomhouse.com

Series Editor Geoffrey Chesler
Design Bobby Birchall

Printed in Malaysia

Cover image: Monument at the top of Santa Lucia Hill, Santiago. *Corbis*

The images on the following pages are reproduced by permission of
the Chilean National Tourist Board, London: 13 (Felipe Orrego);
19, 71 (George Munro); 68, 90, 134, 135, (Norberto Seebach);
66 (SERNATUR), 124 (ClaudioVicuña), 137 (Francisco Tagini),
and 164 (Augusto Dominguez).

The photographs on pages 14, 123, and 132 are reproduced by permission
of Roberto Pagani.

About the Author

CATERINA PERRONE works in the media and information sectors across Europe and Latin America. She holds an M.A. in Translation Studies and Economics from the University of Mainz (Germany) and an M.Sc. in Globalization and Latin American Development from the Institute of the Studies of the Americas (University of London and London School of Economics). She lived in Chile for two years, where she worked both in the business and the nonprofit sectors, and spent months traveling to the most remote corners of the country.

The Culture Smart! series is continuing to expand.
For further information and latest titles visit
www.culturesmartguides.co.uk

The publishers would like to thank **CultureSmart!**Consulting for its help in researching and developing the concept for this series.

CultureSmart!Consulting creates tailor-made seminars and consultancy programs to meet a wide range of corporate, public-sector, and individual needs. Whether delivering courses on multicultural team building in the USA, preparing Chinese engineers for a posting in Europe, training call-center staff in India, or raising the awareness of police forces to the needs of diverse ethnic communities, it provides essential, practical, and powerful skills worldwide to an increasingly international workforce.

For details, visit www.culturesmartconsulting.com

CultureSmart!Consulting and **CultureSmart!** guides have both contributed to and featured regularly in the weekly travel program "Fast Track" on BBC World TV.

contents

contents

Map of Chile

introduction

Chile is famous for its natural beauty—the breathtaking mountain views, inaccessible glaciers, and rugged coast. However, it owes its charm above all to its people: so Latin American, yet so different from any Latino stereotypes.

Remote and beautiful, Chile lies isolated from the rest of the world. This isolation explains the courage, determination, and strong sense of identity of the Chileans, both the native Indians and those migrants who ventured across the seas to settle here. Chileans are proud people; reserved and almost mistrustful at first, they open up with time and are very hospitable. Their geography and, more recently, their political isolation and repression, have had a profound influence on their character; they are more sober and restrained than other Latin Americans.

Chile will surprise those looking for tropical heat, sensuality, and Latin *laissez-faire*. Although its history has much in common with the rest of the continent, it has largely followed its own course, very different from that of its neighbors.

Despite their patriotism, Chileans often see themselves as "provincial" and old-fashioned; they have a strong desire to connect with the rest of the world, hence their interest in foreigners and their fascination with travel. Since the return to democracy in 1989, Chileans have undergone a gradual transformation. Their newly acquired freedom, economic success, and improved living standards have boosted their self-confidence and made them eager to defy traditions and taboos. While still painfully shaking off their traumatic past, they are modernizing at a dizzying speed.

After an initial description of its varied and dramatic geography, *Culture Smart! Chile* focuses on the people, whose ancestors include warlike Indians, ambitious *conquistadores*, and desperate migrants. It describes the core values of Chilean society, in particular the key roles of family, class, and solidarity. It discusses how Chileans relate to each other and establish friendships, explores their attitude toward foreigners, and provides useful tips to help you make the best of your stay. For those visiting on business, there are vital insights into business practices and negotiating style. Finally, it reveals two striking aspects of Chilean culture: the pleasures of Chilean food and the daunting originality of Chilean Spanish. *Culture Smart! Chile* will introduce you to the often surprising charms of a multifaceted and fascinating society.

Key Facts

Official Name	República de Chile	
Capital City	Santiago de Chile (pop. approx. 5 million)	
Major Cities	Valparaíso (pop. 276,000); Viña del Mar (pop. 318,500); Concepción (pop. 216,100); Temuco (pop. 245,350); Valdivia (pop. 140,560); Puerto Montt (pop. 175,940) [source: 2002 census]	
Area	292,300 sq. miles (756,950 sq. km)	
Terrain	Great diversity of landscapes with low coastal mountains, a fertile central valley, and the rugged Andes in the east.	Altitude ranges from sea level to 22,610 ft (6,893 m) at Ojos de Salado. There are 3,999 miles (6,435 km) of coastline.
Climate	Extremely varied: dry in the north; Mediterranean and temperate in the Central Region; cold and damp in the south.	
Currency	Chilean peso (peso chileno). The U.S. dollar sign ($) is used.	Per capita GDP U.S. $11,300 [2005 estimate]
Population	Approx. 16.1 million [2006]	
Life Expectancy	Men 73 years, women 80 years	
Adult Literacy Rate	96.40%	
Ethnic Makeup	95% white or white-Amerindian; 3% indigenous Amerindian. In 2002 over 4% of the population defined themselves as indigenous; of these, over 80% belonged to the main indigenous group, the Mapuche.	

Language	Spanish. There are also a few indigenous languages, such as Rapa Nui on Easter Island, and the Mapuche language, Mapudungun.	
Religion	89% Catholic; 11% Protestant	
Government	Chile is a multiparty democracy with a president (elected for a 4-year term) as head of state and head of government.	
Media	Various national TV channels, incl. the government-owned TVN, the privately owned Canal 13, and Megavisión. Cable and satellite are widely available.	Several national and regional newspapers: *El Mercurio* is the most important daily.
Media: English Language	Various English-language newspapers and magazines	CNN International, Voice of America, and other foreign broadcasters
Electricity	220 volts, 50 Hz AC	U.S. and U.K. appliances need an adaptor.
Telephone	Chile's country code is 56.	Do not add 0 to the local area code.
TV/Video	NTSC system	
Internet Domain	.cl	
Time Zone	Four hours behind Greenwich Mean Time (G.M.T. - 4)	From October to March, G.M.T. - 3 (daylight saving time)

chapter one

LAND & PEOPLE

"After God created the world, he stopped and looked puzzled at all the little pieces that were left. There were lush forests, clear lakes, inhospitable mountains, and fertile plains. He decided to stick them all together and place them right at the end of the world, to make the longest country on earth: Chile."

This legend, which Chileans tell with pride and wit, sums up how they see themselves and their country.

GEOGRAPHY

Chile is a long, narrow stretch of land that runs along much of the Pacific coast of South America. The terrain ranges from sea level to the great Andes mountains, the highest point of which is 22,572 feet (6,880 m). Only 20 percent of its territory is flat. Chile borders Peru in the north, and Argentina and Bolivia to the north and east, and has over 3,700 miles (6,000 km) of rugged coast along the west side. The country can be divided into four main areas: the Andes (commonly called the Cordillera) in the east; the lesser coastal range (the Cordillera de la Costa); the Central Region (the Zona Central); and Patagonia in the south.

The Andes, which start way north in Venezuela, stretch along the entire length of Chile. They are the result of the intense seismic activity caused by the pressure exercised by the oceanic Nazca Plate against the South American Plate. Peaks can reach over 20,000 feet (6,000 m) in the north and center of the country, where they are part of several complex

mountain ranges stretching from east to west. Toward the south the Andes become much lower, in particular in Patagonia and Tierra del Fuego, where they are carved by glacial valleys, deep fjords, and channels. The entire Andean area is characterized by intense volcanic activity. There are over 2,000 volcanoes, some of which are still active.

The coastal range runs from Arica in the north to Puerto Montt at about latitude 42°, taking the form of high vertical cliffs or mountain ranges that rise over 7,000 feet (2,100 m). At this point it continues under the ocean and forms the various archipelagos that dot the southern part of the country. Chiloé is the largest of these islands.

The Central Region is a series of plains situated between the sea and the mountains and consists of two main areas. The Atacama Desert in the north, which extends for over 1,200 miles (2,000 km), is one of the driest areas in the world. The central area in the strict sense of the word lies between Santiago and Puerto Montt; it is the country's most densely populated region and the main agricultural center. Almost 75 percent of the total Chilean population live in the part of this region that lies between Viña del Mar and Concepción and includes the capital Santiago.

Further south lies Chilean Patagonia, a mountainous region shaped by glaciation and volcanic eruptions. Northern Patagonia consists of several islands, coastal mountains, and lakes.

There are only a few towns connected to the north via a very precarious road called the Carretera Austral (or sometimes the Camino Austral). Southern Patagonia is extremely isolated as fjords and glaciers extending across the entire Chilean territory make it accessible only by air or via Argentina. It is a rugged region with a central glacial plain mostly used for cattle and sheep farming. The Magellan Strait separates main

CHILEAN REGIONS

Region	Area	Capital
I* Tarapacá	Norte Grande (The "Big" North)	Iquique
II Antofagasta	Norte Grande	Antofagasta
III Atacama	Norte Chico (The "Small" North)	Copiapó
IV Coquimbo	Norte Chico	La Serena
V Valparaíso	Zona Central (The Central Region)	Valparaíso
VI O'Higgins	Zona Central	Rancagua
VII Maule	Zona Central	Talca
VIII Bío-Bío	El Sur (The South)	Concepción
IX Araucanía	El Sur	Temuco
X Los Lagos	Región de los Lagos (The Lake Region)	Puerto Montt
XI Aisén (also spelled Aysén)	Carretera (also Camino) Austral	Coyhaique
XII Magallanes y la Antártica Chilena	Southern Patagonia & Tierra del Fuego	Punta Arenas
RM Región Metropolitana de Santiago	Santiago & Surrounding Area	Santiago

*Chilean regions are often identified simply by their number.

Patagonia from the island of Tierra del Fuego, a windswept region, flat in the north and mountainous in the south.

Easter Island, discovered by a Dutch explorer on Easter Day and annexed to Chile by treaty, is a volcanic Polynesian island situated almost 2,500 miles

(4,000 km) from Santiago. There are three volcanoes and gentle slopes covered with low vegetation. Unlike other Polynesian islands, which are sheltered by coral reefs, it has a rugged coast with high vertical cliffs eroded by the sea. Chile also claims an area of Antarctica south of Cape Horn.

CLIMATE

Chile is locked between the sea and the Andes, which in the north acts as a barrier against the bad weather fronts coming from Argentina in the east, while further south it traps all the moisture from the Pacific, causing continuous heavy rain. In addition, the Chilean coast is exposed to the cooling effect of the cold Humboldt Current, which flows northward all the way to Ecuador and is responsible for the relatively moderate temperature of northern Chile and the typical ocean mist called *camanchaca.*

Northern Chile has a very dry climate but, despite the latitude, temperatures are never very high. In the desert and at high altitudes, the sun can be extremely hot during the day and there are cold nights. In the Central Region the climate is temperate. It rains more and temperatures range from 50°F (10°C) to around 85°F (30°C). In the south, precipitation is more frequent and heavier, with low temperatures and only sporadic sunny days in summer. This is one of the stormiest and wettest regions on earth. In Patagonia, winters are very cold—40°F (4°C) on average—with snow and frost. In spring and summer, strong westerly winds make the weather extremely changeable, bringing heavy rains from the ocean.

As Chile is in the southern hemisphere, October to March (late spring and summer) is the best time to visit, especially when traveling in the south. November and December might be rainy, but are the best months to enjoy beautiful Chilean flowers, such as *copihues* (the national flower) and fuchsias. February is the holiday month in Chile, so tourist areas should be avoided. The north can be visited throughout the year. In the Andean highlands the driest and sunniest period is in winter (from June to August).

POPULATION

About 95 percent of the Chilean population is of white or white-Amerindian origin. This ethnic composition is the result of Spanish colonization, the subsequent extinction of a large part of the indigenous people, and finally the arrival of immigrants from Europe, the Middle East, and Asia. Despite this complicated history, Chileans feel and like to be thought of as a homogeneous society of European origins. Many value a fair complexion, and look down on an "indigenous" appearance. There is a collective denial of the multiethnic nature of Chilean society, where indigenous communities are largely ignored and marginalized.

Indigenous Groups

Before the arrival of the Spanish in the sixteenth century, the country was inhabited by different Indian groups, some of whom still survive today. Although few Chileans will admit their Indian origins, *mestizaje* (miscegenation) is very common. As a popular saying goes, "There's no Chilean family without an Indian woman hidden somewhere in the family tree." This mixing started in the Spanish communities, which were, at least initially, mainly male; Indian women were often taken as concubines or servants, or simply raped. With time, Spaniards and indigenous peoples intermingled through trade, and in some rural areas, such as the island of Chiloé, they were practically living together.

The Mapuche ("People of the Land"), or Araucanos, as they were called by the Spaniards, are the largest indigenous group in Chile (currently around 600,000 people). Originally they lived between Talca (south of Santiago) and Chiloé; today they are concentrated mainly in the area around Temuco. The Mapuche lived by farming and fishing and were structured around family groups. They resisted the Spaniards ferociously. Although never defeated, they ended up signing a very unfavorable treaty, and gradually lost almost all their land. Now largely marginalized and impoverished, the Mapuche are often the victims of prejudice and abuse. Although legislation has attempted to repair some of the damage, recent protests against timber companies and the construction of a dam threatening their livelihood show that they are still fighting for a

meaningful recognition of their rights. As in all of Latin America, racism toward the *indios* is deeply rooted. Even if you admire a dark complexion and Indian features, be wary of pointing them out to a Chilean—it might not be taken as a compliment!

Smaller indigenous groups can be found in the north and in Patagonia. Today, 48,000 Aymara live in the coastal cities of the north. In Patagonia most Indians were killed either by Spanish and Chilean expansion or by disease, marginalization, and alcohol. The few survivors belong to the Yagan and the Kawashkar.

Immigrants
From the mid-nineteenth century the composition of the population started to change

with the arrival of European immigrants. Chile welcomed them in the belief that white Europeans would bring modernity, progress, and civilization to the country. The British were involved in trade, finance, and the development of the navy and the transport system. German immigration was actively encouraged by the government from 1852, with the aim of populating the areas around Valdivia and the Lake Region. Many Germans emigrated to Chile during or directly after the Second World War. Some were Nazi criminals; others were simply poor refugees fleeing the war.

At the end of the nineteenth century in remote areas such as Patagonia, state-sponsored immigration became the key to consolidating Chilean claims to a strategically important territory. Historically this area had been the object of British, French, Dutch, and, later, Argentinian ambitions. East Europeans, Austrians, and Welsh all migrated here, attracted by gold, cattle farming, and whaling.

In the second half of the twentieth century Chile experienced a wave of immigration from the Arab world (especially from Palestine and Lebanon), and to a lesser extent from China and Korea. Today, a new group of migrants is reaching the country— poor Peruvians who take on low-paid jobs, traditionally the domain of unskilled Mapuche. If you happen to take a stroll in the center of Santiago on a Sunday, you might think you were in Lima.

A BRIEF HISTORY
Colonial Chile

Pre-Hispanic Chile was inhabited by various indigenous peoples. In the fifteenth century the Incas of Peru conquered northern and central Chile, but their expansion was halted by Mapuche opposition south of Santiago. The Inca Empire was already on the verge of collapse when in 1535 the conquistador Diego de Almagro reached Chile. Almagro entered the country from the Andes with an army of Spanish soldiers and African and indigenous slaves. Only six years later, Pedro de Valdivia founded Santiago de Nueva Extremadura, now Chile, and incorporated the country into the Viceroyalty of Peru. Valdivia died fighting the Mapuche, who were only brought under control by the Spanish some two hundred years later.

Despite their great efforts to conquer and subdue this southern region of their empire, the Spanish never saw Chile as a key colonial territory. Its mineral riches had yet to be discovered, and the colony became merely an agricultural center, receiving little attention from Lima. Such isolation, and their reliance on Peru for governance, created discontent among the *criollos* (those Spaniards born in the colony).

Independence and Autocracy

On September 18, 1810, the *criollos* forced the colonial governor to resign, appointed a *junta de gobierno* (governing committee), and declared independence (though this was actually achieved only eight years later). Defeated by the royalists at the "disaster of Rancagua," the republicans fled to Argentina, where they joined the army of José de San Martín and defeated the Spaniards in 1818.

Chile's national hero and first president was Bernardo O'Higgins, the son of an Irish-born former governor and a member of the Spanish aristocracy. In 1823 O'Higgins was forced to resign by the conservative establishment—they could not accept his authoritarian style and, most importantly, his attempts to curb the power of the Church and the landowners.

O'Higgins's successors were unable to prevent conflict between the conservative elite and the Church on one side and the liberals on the other. A general state of anarchy lasted until 1833, when the Conservatives finally gained control and drafted a new constitution, which vested the president with enormous powers. As in the rest of Latin America, the quest for independence was largely driven by the aspiration of the local colonial elites to legitimize their power. José Joaquín Prieto, Manuel Montt, and Diego Portales were some of the prominent politicians of this period, which came to an end in 1861 with the election of a Liberal president.

This phase coincided with the rise of new social groups who were eager to participate in political life. What had been a predominantly agricultural society, where wealth was concentrated in the hands of a few powerful landowners, was gradually being transformed by events in Europe, particularly in Britain. With the Industrial Revolution, Chile started to exploit its natural resources, such as nitrates, guano, and copper, and began intensive export activities.

With trade came investment, new jobs, and new trends. The new elites aspired to limit the power of the president, reform society according to the European liberal model, and reshape politics through Congress. During the Liberal period the government instituted  important reforms such as the separation of Church and state, the introduction of civil marriage, and freedom of religion.

Territorial Expansion and the War of the Pacific
The Liberal period (1861–91) saw the territorial expansion of Chile. Internally, the government ended centuries of Mapuche semiautonomy by forcing the indigenous communities into reservations and selling their land, an initiative that marked the beginning of a series of abuses against the Mapuche. Through organized immigration and the settlement of predominantly German immigrants, Chile also acquired control over the Lake Region and the south. It consolidated its expansion into Patagonia and Tierra del Fuego through a border agreement with Argentina, and finally annexed Easter Island.

The most significant territorial change was, however, the result of a four-year conflict with Bolivia and Peru. Victory in the War of the Pacific (1879–83) enabled Chile to incorporate the northern regions from Antofagasta to Arica and Tacna, although the latter was returned to Peru in 1929. The main reason for the war was economic, as Chile strove to gain full control over its nitrates and copper mines, which were situated in Bolivia. For many years Bolivia had granted mining concessions to Chile; however, disputes arose over Bolivia's constant demands for increases in royalty payments, culminating in Bolivia's ordering the expropriation of the mines. Bolivia felt confident in taking this action because it had just signed a secret alliance with Peru.

The war was fought on sea and land and had disastrous consequences for Peru and Bolivia. Both countries lost economically and strategically important territories. Bolivia lost its only access to the sea. Even today Bolivia contests Chile's rights to the annexed territory, and the conflict lies at the heart of the tense relationships between Chile and Bolivia, and, to a lesser extent, Peru. For Chile, victory brought economic prosperity and military supremacy.

The Oligarchy, the Military, and the New Classes
In 1891, however, Chile's wealth led to a bloody civil war, when the elites opposed President Balmaceda's decision to tax nitrate revenues in order to finance education and other state initiatives. The conflict ended with the president's suicide and the supremacy of the elites, who were able to safeguard their privileges and manipulate elections through parliamentary alliances.

From 1891 to 1925 the country went through a radical transformation, propelled by the export boom in nitrates and copper. While the elites were increasingly accumulating wealth, the Chilean state managed to use some of the export revenues to improve the country's infrastructure and social services. However, this was not enough to provide for the urban poor, who had flocked to the mining areas and the towns in search of work, and who were living in dire conditions, on low salaries increasingly eroded by inflation. At the turn of the century and for years to come, Chilean society was extremely unequal and unstable.

The start of the twentieth century brought the first violent clashes between workers and the state, and the creation of the Chilean Socialist Party. Economic recession following the First World War exacerbated social divisions and forced the Liberals to seek an alliance with the middle class and the workers. This maneuver brought the populist Liberal Arturo Alessandri to power (1920–24) and eventually led to the first military government in the history of Chile. Alessandri's reforms raised social expectations and led to a conservative backlash. The army stepped in to restore order and ended up rigging the elections in favor of the Conservative minister of war, Carlos Ibáñez (1927). Ibáñez suppressed the workers' movements and borrowed from the United States to finance a series of development programs. When the world depression hit Chile, Ibáñez was left with no other resource than repression and he was eventually ousted in 1931.

The Popular Front

The world depression caused a dramatic fall in exports, mass unemployment, and high inflation. Between 1932 and 1938 Alessandri introduced strict financial measures to curb public spending and revive exports. Despite his success in reducing unemployment, he failed to improve workers' wages and alienated the left by stifling protest. In 1938 Communists, Socialists, and the Radical Party, representing the workers and the middle class, formed the Frente Popular (Popular Front) and won the elections, bringing Aguirre Cerda to power.

The Frente Popular, which governed until 1946, broke away from the export model and embarked on state-led development. Chile embraced Latin America's postdepression mantra of import-substitution: instead of relying on highly volatile exports of primary commodities and importing all other goods, thus fueling inflation, a country ought to industrialize and become self-sufficient. Industrialization would create jobs, was not exposed to the fluctuations of the commodity markets, and would ultimately trigger development. According to this economic model, which would be dismantled years later by

Pinochet, the state played a key role in supporting development through investment, import taxes, and the creation of development agencies.

The center-left alliance (1938–46) ruled through a system of compromises aimed at ensuring a general commitment to constitutional order, and kept the armed forces at bay. Power sharing was necessary because the right, the left, and the center had approximately the same number of seats in parliament. The support of the middle class was guaranteed through the creation of white-collar jobs and the granting of subsidies to small industries. Workers were kept relatively under control through nominal wage increases and social benefits. In exchange for progressive reforms in the urban areas, landowners were given a free hand in the countryside, where the peasants were heavily repressed and wages were kept low.

These opportunistic arrangements, however, could not support the center-left alliance for very long. Tensions and strikes increased after the Second World War, when the newly elected president, Gabriel González Videla, froze wages. In response to opposition from the Communists, Videla declared a state of siege and outlawed the Communist Party. The then Communist senator and poet Pablo Neruda was forced to hide and eventually flee the country.

Divisions and the Christian Democrat Government

The 1950s were years of turmoil in Chile. The Frente Popular broke up and the need to create new alliances became stronger than ever. With no support from the alienated left, the Radicals turned to the right, bringing the former dictator Ibáñez back to power. Then the Radicals split internally with the emergence of the Christian Democrat Party and the victory of Jorge Alessandri (1958). Alessandri tried to find a balance between the need to curb inflation and attract foreign capital, particularly from the U.S.A., and the pressure to address the acute social problems arising from industrialization.

By now, Chile's mines were predominantly in the hands of U.S. investors, who kept a large part of the profits and carried out any value-adding processing activities in the U.S.A. Alessandri, while borrowing money from the U.S.A., introduced a law that forced it to refine copper in Chile. Another law confiscated all land lying idle on Chilean landowners' estates. These measures were unpopular both with the right, who wanted to halt the government, and with the left, who wanted outright nationalization of the copper mines and a systematic land redistribution.

This kind of conflict was common throughout Latin America during the period, as the ruling classes fought to maintain their privileges against increasing pressure from the workers and the middle class to share some of their wealth. While its neighbors turned to dictatorship and the eradication of opposition, Chile showed itself able to contain the class struggle within its democratic framework. Still, political stability depended on strategic alliances between the center and the left (as in the Frente Popular) or the right (as in the 1950s). With the emergence of the Socialist Party and its candidate Salvador Allende, the right decided to support the Christian Democrats and their candidate Eduardo Frei.

Frei launched the so-called "Revolution in Liberty," a reform of the state and the economy within the legal democratic framework. Under Frei the government worked with Europe and the U.S.A. to attract capital and foster trade; at the same time it undertook land expropriation and redistribution to the poor peasants. It also acquired some control over U.S.-owned copper mines. However, the government encountered broad opposition: the right opposed its perceived lack of respect for private property, while the left criticized it for its timid reforms. Boosted by the success of the Cuban Revolution, the left was no longer willing to compromise and aimed at taking direct control of power. Pressured from all sides, the Christian Democrats broke up and in 1970

Salvador Allende, the candidate of the new left coalition Unidad Popular, won the elections.

Salvador Allende: the Socialists in Power

The new socialist government faced difficulties right from the start. First, its 36 percent majority forced it to seek alliances in both chambers; such alliances were disliked by the extreme left (MIR), leading to internal divisions. Second, it never managed to gain full control over key state sectors such as the civil service and, above all, the army. Finally, the Chilean socialist experiment soon drew the attention of the U.S. government. Worried about its own economic and strategic interests (it was the peak of the Cold War), the U.S. administration started secretly to fund the Chilean right.

The socialists sought to boost economic growth, redistribute wealth, and create a more equal society, removing the privileges of the oligarchy. Through the nationalization of industry, land redistribution, and state economic planning, Allende aimed to achieve full employment; this would increase purchasing power, stimulate demand, and lead to economic growth. Unfortunately, events unfolded quite differently. After an initial boom, inflation jumped to almost 200 percent. Production was halted by the scarcity of increasingly unaffordable imports, and by disorganization following the large-scale expropriation of private companies. The opposition boycotted the reforms by organizing strikes or slowing down production. At the same time, President Nixon halted all U.S. investment and aid to Chile.

By the fall of 1972 the economic crisis had led to widespread antigovernment street protests and pro-government rallies. Extremists on both sides attempted to destabilize the situation further. With the country on the brink of civil war, Allende desperately tried to keep control of the army and maintain constitutional order. In September 1973, however, his faithful commander-in-chief, General Carlos Prat, who had kept the army in check, resigned. Deprived of his support and without the backing of the alienated center, Allende could do nothing to oppose the coup led by General Augusto Pinochet on September 11, 1973. He died during the army's assault on La Moneda, the presidential palace.

The Military Dictatorship
Once in power, the military set about eradicating all opposition. They governed by decree until 1980,

imposed curfews and restrictions, and violently repressed the opposition, officially sending thousands of Chileans into exile. The country experienced one of the most ruthless dictatorships in the history of Latin America. Aided by the infamous DINA (the Chilean secret police), the government systematically violated human rights. Thousands of people were abducted, tortured, and killed. Some were thrown into the sea or buried in secret mass graves. Although the entire country was affected, the memories of these terrible crimes are associated with two particularly infamous places: Villa Grimaldi, the headquarters of the secret police and scene of the worst atrocities; and the Santiago Stadium, where thousands were detained immediately after the coup.

The military banned all opposition parties and effectively suspended the others by recessing parliament indefinitely. This came as a surprise, because their supporters had expected them to bring the country to order and then hand over power to a civilian government. Instead, Pinochet remained in power for sixteen years.

Human rights abuses were accompanied by harsh economic policies. Determined to revive the economy, Pinochet imposed a program based on free competition, privatization, and cuts in public spending, welfare, and state subsidies. This shift to a free-market economy was executed by the so-called "Chicago Boys," a group of young Chilean economists who had studied at the University of Chicago, the then center of neoliberal economic theory. During the first decade, Chile's economic performance improved substantially, but at a high social cost. Unemployment, for example, rose by over 300 percent, and poverty increased, in particular in the urban shantytowns.

Confident that economic success would provide the military with constitutional legitimacy, Pinochet organized a plebiscite in 1980. He won as the only candidate and ratified a new constitution, extending his mandate for eight more years. This, however, could not hide the increasing discontent of large sections of the population, who, particularly after the 1982 recession, were excluded from the country's economic success and were growing tired of repression.

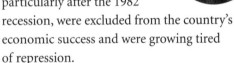

In 1988, one year before the end of his mandate, Pinochet cunningly held another plebiscite, in the hope of remaining in power until 1997. Defeated by 6 percent, and abandoned by sections of the armed forces, he was forced to hold democratic elections. In 1989 the opposition formed an alliance including the center and the left (Concertación de Partidos por la Democracia: see more below) and won the elections with 55 percent of the vote. In March 1990 the Christian Democrat Patricio Aylwin became president, in charge of reintroducing democracy into a highly divided and traumatized Chile.

Democracy Restored

The emergent democracy looked uncertain. It was based on a coalition of groups that were very different and, in some cases, divergent. In addition, the parliamentary opposition represented the very forces that had directly supported the dictatorship but were now incorporated into the democratic process. Even Pinochet was still part of the new Chilean state, first as head of the armed forces, and then from 1998 as senator for life. The sense of precariousness was increased by the divisions created by the Truth and Reconciliation Commission, set up by Aylwin in April 1990 to investigate the crimes committed during military rule. There were also several isolated terrorist attacks aimed at destabilizing the new regime.

Despite this difficult start, democracy prevailed. Its success can be explained by the determination of the majority of Chileans to create an inclusive, peaceful regime that would look to the future to reshape the country. At the same time, Aylwin apologized in the name of the Chilean state for the crimes of the dictatorship and pardoned four left-wing militants who had tried to assassinate Pinochet in 1986.

As the transition had been the result of political agreements, rather than a violent conflict, the government managed to achieve compromises on labor, fiscal, and legal issues. It maintained the free-market economy, which had brought growth and stability, tried to tackle poverty, and committed itself to the goal of social justice.

In the 1993 elections, Concertación again defeated the opposition (today called Alianza por Chile, Alliance for Chile). The new president, Eduardo Frei, presided over the most euphoric period of the new democracy. Between 1992 and 1997 the country experienced an unprecedented economic boom (8 percent). The standard of living rose across the board. Economic growth transformed Chile into a modern consumerist society and fueled it with optimism.

GOVERNMENT

Chile is a presidential democracy. The president is head of the executive and the highest state authority. He is elected directly by the citizens for a four-year term and cannot be reelected. To win, a presidential candidate needs an absolute majority; a second ballot is held if no clear winner emerges in the first round. The Congreso (Senate and Chamber of Deputies) exercises legislative power and is elected directly. Everybody over eighteen has the right to register on the electoral roll. Once registered, Chileans have the duty to vote and also to preside at a polling station if randomly selected. On election day, the entire country follows the *ley seca* ("dry law"): alcohol is prohibited; banks and ATMs are blocked. The thirteen regions are each governed by an appointed *intendente*, and an elected council.

Since 1990 Chile has been governed by the center-left coalition, Concertación; this includes the PDC (Christian Democrat Party), PS (Socialist Party), PPD (Party for Democracy), and PRSD (Radical Social-Democratic Party). The opposition consists of the right-wing and often philo-Pinochet UDI (Independent Democratic Union) and RN (National Renewal).

CHILE TODAY

In 1997, the year that brought an end to the myth of perpetual growth, Chile entered a period of challenge that continues to this day. Lack of competitiveness and a series of external factors, such as the Asian and Brazilian financial crises, 9/11, world recession, and finally the Argentine devaluation, combined to drag the country into a dramatic slowdown. The rise in unemployment and job insecurity signaled that Chile's neoliberal system could not protect its citizens from the vagaries of the market. Above all, and despite many promises, much more needed to be done to achieve a truly egalitarian society, in particular in education, job security, and housing. These issues dominated the mandate of the new socialist president, Ricardo Lagos (1998–2005).

Lagos inherited a country in deep economic crisis. The middle classes felt abandoned by Frei, who, according to some, had prioritized the interests of big business. In addition, Pinochet's arrest in London in 1998 had divided society and brought to the surface the unresolved issue of past responsibilities. Lagos improved the health system and introduced measures to monitor state-run education. During his time in office Chile made advances in family and labor law. In 2001 it explicitly prohibited employers from demanding a pregnancy test as a condition of employment, and in 2004 Chile finally legalized divorce.

Important changes have taken place since 1990. Democracy, economic wealth, and globalization have transformed society: traditional values are being eroded; there is greater social mobility; the family is gradually losing ground. Chile is starting to look more European than Latin American. In 2006, the Chileans took the revolutionary step of voting for a woman president. Although politically Michelle Bachelet does not represent a change from Lagos, the victory of a former victim of the dictatorship and a divorced working woman would once have been unthinkable.

HUMAN RIGHTS AND THE PINOCHET CASE

Chile's new democratic governments have been confronted with the grim task of investigating the atrocities perpetrated by the dictatorship. Initially, the new democracy faced the outright opposition of the army, which justified all its actions, and, indeed, felt protected by the 1978 amnesty that cunningly prohibited the prosecution of abuses carried out between 1973 and 1978 (the most ferocious phase of the regime). The Truth and Reconciliation Commission set up by Aylwin was a step in the right direction, but did not lead to any prosecutions. Today, there has been substantial progress in investigating human rights abuses: cases of disappearances and executions have been reopened and those responsible prosecuted, in particular as a result of evidence gathered by the National Commission on Political Imprisonment and Torture. Many victims are still waiting for compensation and much remains to be done; nevertheless, the country can no longer deny the facts of what took place under Pinochet's regime.

The trigger for change was the detention of Pinochet in London in 1998. The previous year, he had been indicted in Spain for crimes against humanity affecting Spanish nationals who died in the events following the coup of September 1973. The Spanish judge Baltasar Garzón sought his extradition from Britain to stand trial in Spain.

While Britain, Spain, and Chile were deliberating, public opinion in Chile was deeply divided. Demonstrations for and against Pinochet ended when Britain rejected the extradition request on medical grounds. Deemed unfit to stand trial, Pinochet flew back to Chile, where he was welcomed at the airport by cheering supporters. This "victory," however, was merely the first act in his long decline. He would later be deprived of his immunity from prosecution and face several lawsuits, although he managed to avoid prosecution on medical grounds.

In 2006 Pinochet died of a heart attack. However, many judicial cases are still ongoing and it remains to be seen whether the dictator will ever be found guilty for his crimes. His death, which triggered street riots, jubilation, and mourning, showed that Chile continues to be deeply divided. While President Bachelet took the decision not to honor him with a state funeral, thousands rallied in his support.

THE ECONOMY

Chile has been an exporter of minerals since the nineteenth century, and is the world's largest copper producer. Over the last thirty years, the economy has undergone radical reshaping along neoliberal lines. Despite its adverse social effects, this "Darwinian" economic model has created economic stability and efficiency. Chile has restructured its industry, focusing on new exports such as salmon farming, counter-seasonal crops, and timber, and has developed a strong service sector, particularly in financial services.

The key to Chile's success lies in the careful management of its copper revenues. The state has always retained a large part of the mining profits, either through taxation or nationalization. Today, Chile has the most stable economy in Latin America: it is modern, competitive, and operates in a relatively transparent and efficient framework. Despite these gains, some Chileans condemn the overwhelming presence of foreign investors, who, they maintain, have no concern for local communities or the environment.

VALUES & ATTITUDES

Defining the "typical" Chilean is quite a challenge. On the one hand, Chileans are reserved, family-oriented, Catholic, and conservative; and yet they are also fun loving, entrepreneurial, neoliberal, and modern. And there is more: though Chileans can be terribly unpunctual, they respect lines and are considered the "*ingleses de América Latina*" (the English of Latin America). Chile today defies any pigeonholing. It is a dynamic country, where contradictory values and forces, some inherited from the past and others brand-new, some homebred and others global, combine or clash as the expression of a society that is redefining itself and becoming more modern.

According to the Chilean sociologist Eugenio Tironi, Chile has been undergoing a rapid process of modernization since the 1980s. With the reorganization of the economy under Pinochet and the subsequent return to democracy, no aspect of Chilean society has remained unaffected by change. Anyone visiting Chile today should keep this statement in mind and be open to experiencing the many facets of this modern, but still deeply traditional country.

FAMILY

The family plays a central role in Chilean society. As in many other Latin countries, families have an overwhelming influence on the individual, and remain a key reference point throughout one's life. Chilean children and teenagers spend much more time with their parents and relatives than happens in Anglo-Saxon societies. Typically, families have their evening meal together, meet up with grandparents and other relatives almost every weekend, and also spend their holidays together. Relatives visit each other regularly if they live nearby. It is common simply to drop in without prior warning, and, according to some Chileans, to refuse to entertain a visiting relative or miss a family reunion without a plausible excuse would cause great offense.

Chileans are usually extremely affectionate within the family. Family members kiss and hug each other and are particularly fond of children. Children, especially boys, are treated like little kings, and it is not difficult to spot the *regalón*, the spoiled or pampered child, usually the youngest in the family. Young people tend to stay at home until they get married or have to move to another town for work reasons. These close-knit family relations provide Chileans with a sense of security and comfort. They can, however, prevent them from exploring life on their own, as there is often no transition period between living with one's parents and setting up home as a married couple. Obviously, family life varies according to social class: in wealthy families, children are looked after by nannies and spend a longer time at school and doing other activities. In poorer families, on the other hand, children might either spend most of their time with relatives or end up being quite lonely if both parents work.

Such is the importance of the family that not having a "proper" one is automatically seen as a failure in life. Most Chileans believe that it is essential to marry and have children, and tend to look at people who are still single in their thirties with slight pity or disapproval. This attitude can be subtle at first, but often ends up becoming explicit pressure on those who do not or cannot conform to the model of the happy family. Despite recent lifestyle changes, a large number of Chilean women still marry young, and give up their studies or careers to raise children. The new generations are changing, however, and Chile is slowly coming to terms with alternatives to the classic family, such as unmarried couples, single mothers (an old but often denied problem), gay couples, or simply singles or couples with no children. Many of these "nontraditional families" have existed in Chile for years, but have been rejected and widely condemned as improper or even immoral.

APELLIDOS VINOSOS

In colonial times, the dominant class consisted of a small group of wealthy landowners, merchants, and, later, mine owners. Throughout Chile's history, these groups sought to protect their interests and resisted any changes that might undermine their power. Even today, Chile is dominated by a handful of powerful families who control the main companies and, despite recent changes, politics. A controversial book by Hernán Millas Correa, *La sagrada familia* (*The Holy Family*), presents a lucid (though, for some, biased) account of the history of the ten most important families in Chile.

If you read the newspapers or watch the news, you'll hear the same surnames over and over again—the Edwards, owners of the main newspaper *El Mercurio*; Frei and Alessandri, key politicians since independence; and Piñera, including Sebastián Piñera, the powerful entrepreneur and right-wing presidential candidate in 2005. Errazuriz, Undurraga, and other Basque surnames are traditionally linked to the landed oligarchy that became wealthy through wine production, and are still part of the powerful elite today. The Chilean expression "*apellido vinoso*" ("wine surname") refers to the select group of families that, despite recent changes, such as the election of a relative newcomer (Bachelet) as president, still control the country.

Hardly any Chileans would deny that theirs is a highly stratified society. However, not many would openly acknowledge the fact that life is difficult for those who do not have contacts (*pitutos*, see page 141–3) or a "good" surname.

SOCIAL CLASSES

Traditionally, Chile has had limited social mobility. Despite the presence of a strong middle class, Chileans tend not to mix with people from other income groups. The upper class and wealthier middle class keep to themselves in the northern boroughs of Santiago (see Chapter 5) and hardly ever go to the center or to the busy downtown districts. Wealthy children attend exclusive schools and universities, and network only with their peers. At home, they might have a glimpse of a different society through the presence of nannies and other servants; however, mixing with children from other classes is the exception rather than the rule. The importance of class is reflected in the number of Chilean words used to describe someone's social position. A few examples are *cuico, pituco, esnob* for upper-class people; *roto, ordinario, flaite* for the lower class. Class divisions are further strengthened by the strong family ties mentioned earlier. A Chilean friend admits that family pressure can prevent one from socializing or marrying outside one's milieu.

Since the 1990s Chilean society has become more fluid. Improved education, economic growth, and the restoration of democracy have all contributed to the growth of the middle class and the emergence of a new group of wealthy Chileans. While the middle class is becoming more open and inclusive, economic success is still not enough to reach the top of the social ladder. Exclusive clubs and insider circles are the ultimate barrier to newcomers who do not enjoy the privilege of a prestigious family tree.

THE CHURCH

Chile is a predominantly Catholic country. As in other former Spanish colonies, Roman Catholicism was introduced in the sixteenth century and since then the Chilean Church has been extremely powerful and a faithful ally of the traditional elite. This alliance has helped make Chile one of the most conservative countries in Latin America and a stronghold of Catholicism. Although the Church under Cardinal Raúl Silva Henríquez played a key role in opposing Pinochet's regime, when democracy was restored it returned to its old role as the defender of traditional values and the main ally of the conservative forces.

The power of this alliance is demonstrated by the recent public debates over divorce, abortion, birth control, and film censorship. After more than a century of political battles, Chile only legalized divorce in 2004. Abortion, however, is still illegal, and a recent decision of the center-left government to distribute morning-after pills in medical centers encountered the opposition of the Church and was boycotted by some local mayors. In 2003, three of the national TV channels refused to broadcast a government anti-AIDS campaign, while Scorsese's controversial film *The Last Temptation of Christ* was banned for many years, until Chile was forced by a ruling of the Inter-American Court of Human Rights to reform its censorship legislation.

In the 2002 census, 75 percent of Chileans gave their religion as Catholic. This does not imply, however, that they all endorse the conservative stance of the national Church. Many Chileans express very modern views and would like to see a change in Church attitudes; others even reject the Church altogether.

A DIVIDED COUNTRY

According to the sociologist Carlos Huneeus, the country is still divided and scarred by the traumatic experience of the dictatorship. His recent study shows that more than 30 percent of Chileans still approve of the 1973 coup and consider Pinochet a great politician. During Pinochet's arrest in London, Chile was torn by protests, both for and against his detention. There is still a heavy presence of *pinochetistas* among the upper class, the army, and some right-wing sections of the lower and middle class who associate the Pinochet regime with economic stability and security. Even today, any conversation about the country's political past or the present investigation of human rights abuses is likely to reveal this polarization within Chilean society.

The sixteen years of dictatorship changed Chile profoundly. Curfews and the suppression of public debate and civic activity largely depoliticized society. Although not all Chileans were directly affected by the repression, the climate of fear changed people's behavior. Nightlife came to a halt, street life was reduced to a minimum, and people became much less talkative and spontaneous. Friends met at home rather than outside, and Chilean hospitality was restrained by fear. Finally, class divisions were exacerbated. The neoliberal economic model contributed further to the erosion of traditional communal ties, encouraging individualism, competition, and ultimately a consumerist society. On the other hand, the challenges posed by the regime fostered a sense of solidarity within the family or among close friends. Since the return of democracy, Chile has seen the emergence of new, wider forms of social solidarity, especially in defense of the victims of the dictatorship and support for the poor.

UNDERSTATEMENT IS KEY

One glance at the elegant areas of Santiago—El Bosque, La Reina, or Vitacura—reveals another intriguing aspect of Chilean society. Chileans prefer to play everything low-key. While upper-class Brazilians, Colombians, and Argentinians sport exclusive cars, designer labels, and all the latest gadgets, Chileans are generally austere and sober. They do not indulge in excess—or at least, so they say—but they value a good education, large villas hidden behind high walls, "proper" behavior, and a "good" accent. Glamour or ostentation are more evident among the new rich, those who have benefited from the recent economic booms, and media celebrities, both frowned upon by the traditional elite.

Traditionally, Chileans are more restrained than other Latin Americans. They avoid speaking in a loud voice and value self-control and the respect of one's privacy. They are also much less liberal than some of their Latin counterparts, such as the Brazilians. "Adult magazines" are never on obvious display, and TV shows with scantily dressed women are hardly ever broadcast during prime time. Chileans don't have a "tropical" temperament, and certainly don't match the stereotype of wild Latin dancers.

GENDER RELATIONS

Since the 1990s the percentage of women completing university studies has increased substantially, as has the number of women working outside the home. Chile still has a long way to go to catch up with European or U.S. levels, but women have certainly seen positive changes. Democracy has also brought important legal changes to safeguard their position. Since 1992 parliament has passed laws against domestic violence, prohibited pregnancy tests as a condition of employment, and introduced some measures to help working mothers. Today,

Chilean women have gained in confidence and freedom. They work in key sectors of the economy and have gradually acquired importance in national politics. Chile's new woman president, Michelle Bachelet, has given important posts to female politicians and is expected to contribute to the advancement of Chilean women.

All these changes represent significant progress in a country that, with its conservative values, has always been quite discriminatory toward women. While the situation has improved, however, *machismo* is still prevalent. First of all, the greatest advances affect mainly the upper and middle classes. Women from the lower classes (many of whom are single mothers) have benefited less from the improvements in education and salaries. A Chilean HR director believes that, despite the rosy picture represented by the statistics, women are still discriminated against. They earn significantly less than their male counterparts and have fewer career opportunities.

Machismo, many Chileans say, goes beyond statistics and recent advances. It is about the freedom that some married men grant themselves while expecting their wives to stay at home. Chilean men can be very jealous and protective, sometimes even keeping tabs on their wives. Some believe that Chilean women are equally guilty of fostering *machismo*: they spoil their sons, and are the first to disapprove of a woman who is not behaving traditionally. Foreign women may be criticized for sharing an apartment with men or having male friends. Today, these views are being challenged by the younger generation of men who help out at home and support their wife's career, and by women who go out alone and have learned to enjoy their independence.

SOLIDARITY AND SUPPORT

Chileans are generally helpful and hospitable. Especially in the countryside, they will go out of their way to help each other. Traditionally, the community and the family played a key role in supporting their weakest members. Such forms of solidarity are still present in the countryside and in the poorest urban boroughs. For example, if someone gets married, the circle of friends might *hacer una minga*, in other words, get together to prepare the flowers, organize the food, or sing. The Quechua expression *minga* is used in many Latin American countries to indicate a team effort of some sort, but *mingas*, in the original meaning of communal work, are still common practice on the island of Chiloé, where families rely on their neighbors' support for major work in the fields. Afterward, the family will show its appreciation by providing a large meal, with dancing and extra food for the guests to take home.

BUREAUCRACY AND PROFESSIONALISM

Chile has the reputation of being one of the most "correct" and law-abiding Latin American countries. Chileans take pride in doing things according to the rules, and this is particularly reflected in the general transparency and honesty of civil servants and the police. A downside may be the Chilean obsession with bureaucracy, receipts, regulations, and signage. Chile, for example, is particularly strict about recognizing foreign professional qualifications, and any foreigner trying to work in the country knows the sheer amount of *trámites* (paperwork) needed in order to be allowed to exercise their profession.

Bureaucracy is also visible in everyday life. In Chile, there is a receipt for everything— *comprobante, vale, recibo, boleta*: the name varies according to the type of transaction. In all shops except supermarkets and some shopping malls, the sales process is bureaucratic and long-winded and involves dealing with at least three members of staff. A sales assistant shows you the goods, fills out a form that is handed to a cashier, and passes your purchase to the *empaque* (wrapping area).

The cashier charges you and issues a receipt, which you then have to present to the *empaque* to retrieve your purchase. In a way, this is another example of the Chilean obsession with *papeleo* (paperwork) and administration. According to some people, it is a good way of creating jobs; for others, it is an example of a hierarchical work culture that shows little trust in its employees and doesn't know how to delegate.

The Chileans seem to love public notices and rules. You will spot many signs inviting pedestrians to keep the streets clean, and numerous safety warnings. Signs are always extremely formal and polite, and address the public as *Estimado peatón* (Dear pedestrian) or *Señor turista* (Mr. tourist). In reality, this respect for rules and laws is often more form than substance. As the sociologist Jorge Larraín points out, Chileans mostly respect the law, but this does not prevent them from ignoring or bending it when it suits them.

Chileans are trustworthy, and their admiration for professionalism, precision, and efficiency makes them very organized and safety conscious. Buses leave on time, national parks are generally well maintained, and Chile's firemen are not only a source of national pride, but are famous throughout Latin America.

ATTITUDES TO FOREIGNERS

Chileans are very eager to travel and discover new countries. Many dream of studying or working abroad, especially in the U.S.A., and there is a general fascination with life outside Chile. U.S. models have been widely adopted: shopping malls, fast food, pickup trucks, and gadgets. English is the cool language of marketing: many advertising slogans are in English, and the owner of a popular pizza chain ensures that young Chileans want pizza "slices," and not *trozos*! Despite this, U.S. visitors may encounter Chileans who have reservations about their country, as memories of U.S. control of Chilean copper mines or support for the former dictatorship are still vivid in their minds.

Most Chileans admit that they are fascinated by non-Latin foreigners, particularly if they have blue eyes and blond hair. Blond babies are prized in Chile, while a dark Indian complexion may be viewed with contempt. Although such attitudes cannot be generalized, one cannot deny the existence of discrimination against indigenous groups and poorer Latin American immigrants from Peru and Bolivia.

Talking about Chilean clichés and prejudices brings one inevitably to Chile's complicated relationship with its neighbor, Argentina. No Chilean will refuse to comment on the

Argentinians, revealing a complex mixture of admiration and contempt. The two countries were on the brink of war in 1978, due to a border dispute in the Patagonian region. The Argentinians' reputation as the "Europeans of Latin America," together with their rather loud and theatrical style, have often generated resentment among Chileans and led to negative stereotyping. On the other hand, the rather low-key and reserved Chileans often look up to their stylish neighbors, seen as beautiful, charming, and cultivated. Recently, as economic growth in Argentina gave way to disarray and eventually recession, this view was tinged with sympathy and affection.

DESTAPE

Two events are often cited as signs of change in Chilean society. The first was an art installation in January 2000: the *Casa de Vidrio* was a transparent glass house placed in the center of the capital, in which a young actress lived for two weeks, revealing even intimate aspects of her daily routine to curious *santiaguinos*. The second event took place in 2002, when over five thousand Chileans gathered in a city park to be photographed naked by Spencer Tunick.

The controversial Glass House was an unprecedented attempt to lay bare the double standards of Chilean morality. The city that publicly accepts cafés where coffee is served by half-naked women (see *café de piernas* below) was shocked by the explicitness of the installation. Critics talked about a repressed and conservative society—an image that in the second event Chileans from all backgrounds were determined to defy by posing naked in front of an American photographer.

These two events have been seen as symbols of the Chilean transformation. Yes, Chileans are conservative, respectful of authority, and Catholic, but they are opening up, becoming more liberal and much less politically correct. The Chilean *destape* (literally, "taking off the lid") has been compared to the opening up of post-Franco Spain. In reality it is less radical, but many Chileans are now defying tradition and convention, and do not fail to point out how proud they are of this newly gained confidence.

THE *CAFÉ DE PIERNAS*

In the center of Santiago there is a unique type of café, following a tradition that is now some forty years old. The *cafés de piernas* (*piernas* means "legs") are stand-up bars where customers are served by scantily dressed waitresses. In these cafés the bar is open fronted, so that the male clientele can admire the waitresses' legs, set off by old-fashioned high-heeled shoes and flesh-colored tights, and reflected by cleverly angled mirror walls. Waitresses spend time chatting up customers, who in turn leave generous tips. On a lucky day patrons can even experience the *minuto milenario*, a sixty-second striptease.

While in the older bars, such as the Café Haiti, waitresses wear a decent short dress, in the newer establishments they are so scantily dressed that the shop windows are darkened. Some bars are suspected of being fronts for prostitution, but these allegations have never been proved. The *cafés de piernas* reveal a specific trait of Chilean culture, which is essentially conservative, puritanical, and still relatively attached to the idea of male dominance, that is, *machismo*. However, the more traditional and decent *cafés de piernas* are a reminder of what Chile used to be like; their old-fashioned seventies style makes them look almost amusingly *passé*. Middle-aged customers in their suits and ties come here perhaps to find the comfort, self-confidence, and security that today's Chile, and in particular today's Chilean women, can no longer give them.

REGIONAL AND RACIAL DIFFERENCES
In Chile, social class is more important than which geographical region you come from, and

santiaguinos will often tell you that there is no difference between them and people from outside the capital (nor any prejudice toward them). Seen through the eyes of the rest of Chile, things are rather different. The further you go from Santiago, the more people differ from the city dwellers. In the southern regions, Chileans often feel abandoned by the state and completely ignored by their compatriots in the larger towns.

In reality, people from the different regions hardly know each other. There is no interchange unless one moves to Santiago, where 35 percent of the population is currently concentrated. There is no regional hostility, however, and the only pejorative cliché you might hear is "He's a *huaso*" (a *huaso* is the traditional Chilean cowboy), referring to the naive and unsophisticated rural Chilean who speaks with a very strong accent and struggles to adapt to life in the city.

Sadly, the indigenous groups are the victims of much stronger prejudice. As we have seen, for many years Chile ignored the presence of its more than one million indigenous people. The Aymara, the Rapa Nui, and the largest group, the Mapuche, were excluded from society, and forced to give up their land and migrate to the cities. Even today, skin color coincides with a social divide. Indigenous people have low-paid jobs and live in the poorest boroughs. Their surnames and appearance are a real obstacle when trying to get a better job. Racism is generally hidden, as many Chileans simply deny it, insisting that theirs is a homogeneous society. Today, such attitudes are slowly changing, due partly to the recent Mapuche protests in defense of indigenous rights, and partly to the national debate provoked by the arrival of poor immigrants from Peru and Bolivia.

chapter three

CUSTOMS & TRADITIONS

Although Chile's customs and traditions predominantly reflect its Spanish and European heritage, they have also been influenced by the encounter with indigenous rituals and their link with the natural world. Today, many traditions are confined to the countryside. Urban Chileans have adopted modern ways and actively celebrate only a few national festivities. They may even be unaware of their own folklore, and prefer to celebrate "imported" festivities such as Halloween.

The Mapuche, the Easter Islanders, and some indigenous groups from the northern regions still follow their traditional customs, although, in some cases, this attachment to ancestral practices is driven more by the desire to preserve their traditions than a real belief in them, as the new generations increasingly embrace a mainstream way of life. Whatever the reason for a traditional festivity, Chileans love to party. They dance, drink, and eat, and invite everybody to join in.

FESTIVALS AND HOLIDAYS

The main Chilean festivities are Christmas, New Year, and the *Fiestas Patrias* (Independence Day and Armed Forces' Day).

Christmas

Christmas is traditionally celebrated with large family gatherings, usually involving a substantial meal. On Christmas Eve Chileans attend the *misa del gallo* (midnight mass) and open presents. On Christmas Day, the family meet for a large *asado* (barbecue), drink *cola de mono* (a sweet, coffee-based alcoholic drink), and eat *pan de pascua*, a cake similar to Italian panettone. In the countryside, preparations for Christmas may even include the purchase of a live lamb, which is kept in the backyard and slaughtered just before the celebrations. On Christmas Day the whole family travels to the countryside and organize an *asado al palo* (roast lamb on a spit; see pages 107–8).

On December 24 and 25, Chile practically shuts down, including most restaurants and bars; the 26th is a normal working day. Cities put up Christmas decorations and shops play Chilean Christmas jingles, but the décor is generally low-key with the exception of shopping malls. Churches have cribs where children can leave "wish cards."

New Year

New Year celebrations usually start at home, where the family have a late meal, typically including seafood. Shortly before midnight, people take glasses of sparkling wine and gather outside to view the midnight fireworks. If you are in Santiago, this can be a chaotic and rather overwhelming experience, as *santiaguinos* try to make their way along jammed roads to reach their favorite vantage points. At midnight everybody cheers, groups break up, and people hug each other. Many people gather in the center of Santiago, where the main fireworks display is held; however, there are several other shows around the city. Valparaíso has Chile's most spectacular fireworks, which are fired from the sea all along the bay. Millions of Chileans travel to the city for the occasion. After midnight, most people go to the various parties held in discos and bars and lasting till morning.

Chileans celebrate various rituals that are meant to bring good luck and prosperity for the New Year. Although there are many regional variations, these are the most common. Like some Southern Europeans, Chileans eat lentils and fruit to bring abundance and wealth. They also drop a gold ring or twelve wine grapes into a glass of champagne before drinking it. Women traditionally wear yellow underwear. Some people go around the block with a suitcase or put a bus ticket in their pocket in the hope of having a new year full of travel. More rural traditions include hanging a bunch of twelve ears of wheat behind the front door, storing wheat in three jars mixed with salt, sugar, and garlic respectively, and sweeping the house to banish negative events from the past year.

Fiestas Patrias

On September 18 and 19, Chile celebrates Independence Day (also known as *el Dieciocho*, the Eighteenth) and Armed Forces' Day. These two festivities commemorate the declaration of independence of 1810, although independence was actually achieved only in 1818. The *Fiestas Patrias* (literally, "national festivities") celebrate *chilenidad* (Chilean national identity) in a sort of collective euphoria that rediscovers traditions and memories that are no longer part of Chilean life. Celebrations start days before the 18th with a series of parades, traditional folk dances, and large quantities of alcohol and food. On the 19th Chile commemorates its national heroes with military parades. Chileans usually start celebrating at home with an *asado* and continue the party in a *ramada*, an open-air venue with a dance floor and food stalls (*fondas*). The country is seized with frenzy and all the media compete to provide the public with, yet again, the best advice on how to grill meat, avoid food poisoning, and dance the traditional dances. Throughout the country, celebrations include Chilean rodeos, sack races, or greasy pole contests and other traditional games.

The 18th is above all the day of the *cueca*, the national dance (see more below), which many Chileans learn at school and dance only on this day. In typical Chilean style, the party does not stop when the holiday comes to an end, but is resumed the following weekend in an unofficial celebration called *el Dieciocho chico* (the small Eighteenth)!

There are many other festivities, some of which are celebrated only in specific regions or towns. Chileans tend to take advantage of these special days to *hacer un puente* (literally, "make a bridge"), that is, attach some extra days of vacation to the official holiday.

Semana Santa (Holy Week)

Easter is celebrated with processions, a family meal, and colored eggs. The first Sunday after Easter, some Chileans celebrate a unique religious ritual known as *Cuasimodo*. Dating back to colonial times, *Cuasimodo* was a procession of priests and *huasos* (traditional Chilean cowboys) bringing Holy Communion to people who were too old or ill to attend mass. The *huasos*, who would wear their formal outfits for the occasion, were in charge of protecting the priests from robbers. This tradition still continues in Chile today, though in a slightly modernized version, which includes carts, bicycles, and motorbikes and has replaced the traditional ponchos with capes. The most popular processions take place in the Central Region and in Colina, a Santiago suburb, where over 3,500 mounted *cuasimodistas* parade with the mayor and the priests.

In Valparaíso and a few other towns, children maintain the tradition of the *quema de Judas* (burning of Judas). Children go around the streets asking for money, which they hide in a puppet stuffed with straw. The puppet is then hanged on the street and burned to avenge Judas's betrayal of Christ.

La Tirana

This religious festival takes place between July 12 and 18 in a small village in northern Chile near Iquique, where thousands of pilgrims congregate to dance and make offerings to *Nuestra Señora del Carmen de La Tirana*, Our Lady of Tirana. The

history of the cult dates back to the sixteenth century, when a missionary discovered a cross and linked this discovery with the local legend of a beautiful pagan tyrant who converted to Catholicism. Tirana de Tamarugal was an Inca princess, who, after witnessing the atrocities committed by the Spaniards, who had murdered her father, vowed to kill any Catholic who came into her community. This hatred continued until Tirana fell in love with a miner, Vasco de Almeyda, and she converted to Christianity. Eventually, the lovers were both killed by the Indians and buried where she was baptized.

San Pedro and San Juan

On June 29, many fishing villages celebrate San Pedro (St. Peter), the patron saint of fishermen.

The saint's image is taken by boat for a procession on the sea.

In many regions people attribute importance to San Juan's Day, June 24. It is a popular belief that San Juan (St. John) brings good luck or can reveal one's destiny. After celebrating him with a large meal, several tricks can be tried to interrogate the saint as to the future. One consists in dropping some ink on four pieces of paper, folding them, and putting them under one's pillow at midnight. The following day the shapes taken by the ink will reveal one's future.

CHILOÉ, ISLAND OF LEGENDS

Most native Chilean mythology originated on the island of Chiloé, where the indigenous Huilliche culture blended with the Spanish and Catholic presence. *Chilote* legends and mythical figures are inspired by the inhospitable and beautiful nature of the region, the sea, and the mysterious forests, feared and loved by the islanders as the providers of food and comfort. The myths convey a strong vision of good and evil, which are represented by semi-human figures like the *traucos*, ugly and deformed gnomes who live in the woods. Despite the *trauco*'s repellent appearance, he charms any woman who happens to wander through the woods alone. His aim is to enter her dreams and steal her virginity.

La Pincoya is a beautiful siren who personifies the sea and dances on the shore or on the waves. When she dances facing the sea, she brings abundance. Should she face the land, then the *chilotes* will endure hunger and misery.

The mystery of the sea and memories of pirates and foreign raids lie at the roots of the most original myth, that of the *caleuche*. This is an enchanted ship that sails the waters around Chiloé. Its crew consists of demoniac and deformed sailors, witches, and those unfortunate enough to have fallen prey to the ship's enchanting music. It is a popular belief that those who have accumulated wealth very quickly have made a pact with the *caleuche*. The *chilote* writer Francisco Coloane provides a beautiful record of this rich mythology and a sober analysis of his rural and superstitious island in his book, *El camino de la ballena* (*The Wake of the Whale*).

Chiloé is also famous for its music and dances, which are performed during religious festivities and as a tourist attraction during the high season.

THE MAPUCHE

The original inhabitants of Chile, the Mapuche, are the repository of the country's indigenous wisdom. However, because they have been marginalized, their traditions and beliefs have had a very limited influence on the national culture. Despite the richness of Mapuche traditions, therefore, the average visitor is unlikely to be exposed to them.

One of the most intriguing Mapuche myths explains the creation of the world. It is startlingly similar to the biblical account of the Flood, and tells of the conflict between the spirits of Earth and Sea, represented by two snakes. When Cai-Cai threatened to open up the seas and flood all the land, Ten-Ten warned its people to seek refuge in the mountains. To fight the fury of the Sea, Ten-Ten created mountains, whose peaks could almost touch the sky, and helped people to escape by turning them into birds. Those who could not escape were turned into fish and stones, and plains were turned into canals and lakes.

Like many indigenous peoples, the Mapuche believe in the forces of nature. The *machis* (female shamans) use herbs, magic, and the sound of the *kultrun* (round drum) to cure illness and predict the future. Typical Chilean herbal infusions such as *boldo* are inspired by the traditional remedies used by the *machis*. Today, these are sold in Makewelawen, a new chain of Mapuche drugstores found in Santiago and throughout central Chile.

Finally, the Mapuche are famous for their
beautiful silver jewelry, their textiles, and their
traditional musical instruments, now produced
mainly as souvenirs for tourists.

TRADITIONAL DANCES

The *cueca* is the national dance of Chile and is
accompanied by guitar, accordion, and
tambourine. It simulates the courtship of a very
difficult woman, who refuses the advances of the
man who stubbornly tries to get closer and closer
to her. The dancers hold a handkerchief to
emphasize their movements. The *cueca* is believed
to have derived from the Peruvian *marinera,* and
resembles the movements of a hen and a rooster,
just like the rather more sensuous Cuban rumba.

Group dances from northern Chile follow the
Andean tradition. Dancers wear colorful costumes
and are accompanied by wind instruments and
percussion, as in the Peruvian and Bolivian
highlands.

Easter Island dances have a completely different
character. The *sau sau* and *ula ula* are the most
famous. They are sensuous with a South Sea
island feeling. In the *sau sau* dancers wear
necklaces made of flowers and shells. This
distinctive and graceful dance is executed by
moving the hips and the arms.

KEY FESTIVITIES

Date	Festival
January 1	New Year's Day
March/April	Easter Week
May 1	Labor Day
May 21	Naval Battle of Iquique
May/June	Corpus Christi
June 24	San Juan
June 29	San Pedro
August 15	Assumption
1st Monday in September	Day of National Unity*
September 18	Independence Day
September 19	Armed Forces' Day
October 12	Columbus Day
November 1	All Saints' Day
December 8	Immaculate Conception
December 25	Christmas Day

*Replaces the contentious celebration of September 11 (the 1973 military coup).

MAKING FRIENDS

Centuries of isolation between the mountains and the sea have helped to create a culture that is atypical on the Latin American continent. Chileans tend to be reserved by nature, though this is usually softened by friendliness and hospitality. Give them time and they will open their house to you and help you in any way they can.

THE FIRST CONTACT

In Chile you will need to make an effort to establish friendships. People will be polite, correct, but will seldom be the first to address you. Young people may behave differently, and some might approach you to practice their English. Some men may be more forthcoming when they spot a single woman traveler, but these are just the exceptions. The majority of Chileans tend to be quite conscious of privacy. Don't be put off by the expression the "English of Latin America," as Chileans jokingly describe themselves. Once approached, they are usually very friendly and talkative. For greetings and forms of address, see pages 155–7.

If you travel outside Santiago, you will encounter some regional differences. In the rural areas of the north, people are similar to the Andean Bolivians: introverted, serious, and slightly mistrustful. Along the coast and in the central metropolitan areas they are more open, although in Santiago urban mistrust can prevail. Southern Chileans, in particular those from the countryside, are renowned for being very approachable and affectionate; still, the first impression will be one of circumspection and distance.

Meeting people is not very difficult. If you work in the country, colleagues will normally invite you for lunch or for a drink after work. If you find it difficult to go beyond your circle of foreign friends or you are completely new to Chile, try joining local associations like sports clubs or evening classes, and using any opportunity to approach people in shops, markets, and tourist attractions. The Chile Information Project (CHIP) has an excellent Web site and provides an extensive list of nonprofit, expatriate, and church organizations (www.chipsites.com/ww/chile_orgs_and_culture.html). Chileans are fascinated by foreigners and, despite their sense of privacy, are usually open to making new contacts. They will often try to talk to you in English; however, the conversation may be constrained by the language difficulty. Don't be put off if you are referred to as the *gringo* or *gringa*—this doesn't usually have any negative connotations.

An easy way to start a conversation is to talk about Chile. Ask about the country and its customs, show an interest in the other person's city or region, and they will quickly warm to you. However, remember that initially Chileans do not easily volunteer any personal information. If asked, they will certainly talk about themselves, but they will hardly ask you any personal questions. Enjoy their warmth and hospitality, but be aware that it takes time for them to open up.

The most frequent exception to this rule is a Chilean man trying to chat up a foreign woman, when the Latin spirit suddenly comes into play. Chileans tend to pay romantic compliments (*piropos*) and become uncharacteristically nosy. Women travelers, especially when venturing into rural and therefore traditional areas, should be prepared to deal with the following questions: "Do you have children?" "Are you married?" "Do you have a boyfriend?" A "no" to the first question triggers the next one and so on. Admitting to being a single woman gives the man a reason to become more romantic or insistent. Female travelers shouldn't be surprised if they are asked similar questions by Chilean women and receive pitying looks if they say they are single.

A FEMALE PERSPECTIVE

If you are a foreign woman and are invited out by a Chilean man, don't be surprised if he volunteers to pay for everything and insists on escorting you home. Equally, if you are a foreign man inviting a Chilean woman out, you should be clear about her general expectations. Chilean women do very occasionally offer to pay, but you should not accept if you want to make a good impression on a first date. Be aware that, although the new generations are slowly changing, inviting a woman out for dinner or accepting a dinner invitation from a man is usually associated with more than just friendship. You could find yourself in an awkward situation, especially if the Chilean fancies you! So try to avoid any misunderstanding. As Isabel Allende reminds us in her book *My Invented Country*, Chileans are very determined when they set their sights on someone and become very demanding when they are dating. *Pololear* (dating) with a Chilean can be quite overwhelming if you are used to independence. Chileans are extremely affectionate and supportive, but can be very possessive and expect your full attention.

Chileans believe in marriage and children, and as we have seen, can struggle with the Western attitude to family. For some, being single equates to being a poor, lonely soul. If you live on your own, you might be deluged with invitations, as friends try to provide you with the family warmth they believe you are missing. It might be difficult to extricate yourself, so if you feel you are getting too much attention and pampering, be very tactful when refusing invitations so as to avoid giving any offense or misunderstanding. The sense of family is so strong in Chile that many people find it inconceivable that someone might prefer to spend time on their own.

DEVELOPING A FRIENDSHIP

As in other traditional societies with low social mobility and strong family ties, establishing friendships in Chile can prove difficult for those foreigners who stay longer. Many foreign visitors find that contacts are easier to make at the beginning, when one is new to the country and somehow "interesting." Those who settle in Chile can experience difficulty in breaking into close-knit social circles. Chileans tend to make friends through school and family. As they often meet in their homes, family acceptance is very important, and friends generally belong to the same social class. Outside their homes and families, friends meet by organizing *asados* in the countryside, planning joint weekend trips, or spending summer vacations at the same resort. Marriages bring the families of both parties closer, and the circle of friendships normally widens to incorporate the partners' friends. Beyond this, Chileans generally do not feel the need to venture outside their circle and meet new people.

For this reason, many foreigners find it difficult to form real friendships with adult Chileans. Some feel that, after an initial enthusiasm, the Chileans then retreat into their "club" and never really admit the outsider. This happens especially among the upper class, where social circles can be harder to break into. However, Chileans who have traveled or studied abroad can be more open and inclusive toward foreigners than toward their own compatriots, who are often excluded on the basis of their social status. Foreigners, in a way, are classless, and can easily have friends across the spectrum, a luxury enjoyed by only a handful of Chileans.

Although foreigners can float above class, matters become trickier if they have a Chilean partner. A German friend who had just announced her forthcoming marriage to a

Chilean was very surprised when colleagues and friends bombarded her with questions all aimed at positioning her future husband on the social scale. The fiancé's surname, profession, address, school, and even his parents' professions were all key information in building his "social identikit."

The Importance of Slang

A good knowledge of Spanish is clearly a great advantage when trying to socialize; however, Chilean and Spanish are slightly different at times, so don't be frustrated if fluent *Castellano* doesn't open all doors. A well-traveled Chilean friend points out that, while he enjoys going out alone with his foreign acquaintances, he hardly ever invites them when he meets his long-standing friends. Friendship among Chilean men, he says, often revolves around jokes, innuendo, and slang. Having a nonnative speaker in the group would mean either excluding him from most of the conversation or feeling constrained by his presence. You could obviously surprise your Chilean acquaintances by learning some slang; not an easy task, however, as you'll see in Chapter 9.

Interestingly, Chileans who have lived in the U.S.A. or the U.K. say that they found it difficult to socialize in these countries, and often experienced loneliness and a lack of support. They felt that friendships were much harder to develop than in Chile, and missed the family network (although some enjoyed the freedom from it as well!). They liked the fact that social classes mix more, that people can be more open, and also that men and women have a more equal relationship. However, their contacts were limited to the workplace or the university and very seldom developed beyond work or study, or it took a long time before they did. They were particularly shocked by the fact that friends do not call or see each other regularly, and families are hardly involved.

When in Chile, put yourself in the Chileans' shoes. To find real Chilean friends you will need to phone and possibly meet up frequently, and accept the support they give you. Consider yourself honored if you are invited to meet the family, as this is a great sign of friendship.

INVITATIONS HOME

Although younger people tend to go out to bars and discos, Chileans usually meet at home either for dinner or for parties with music and dancing. They also invite friends for *once* (pronounced "on-say"), or afternoon tea (see pages 105–6). On weekends some people organize *asados*, which can either be held in the garden or be combined with a trip to the countryside. The wealthiest often drive out of Santiago to a holiday house. When invited for dinner, bring flowers for the hostess and a bottle of wine or a cake. If you are invited for a weekend out in the country, choose a more substantial gift, for instance a decorative object for the house.

TIMEKEEPING

Whatever is stated on the invitation, starting times should be taken with a grain of salt! Never turn up on time as nobody will be expecting you. Chileans have a flexible attitude toward punctuality: they are normally on time for business meetings, but half an hour to one hour late for social events.

If you are meeting someone outside their home, try not to be late the first time, in case you are dealing with an exceptionally punctual Chilean (or one who knows that foreigners are punctual). Choose a comfortable and safe meeting point, such as a café, to avoid being stranded on the street waiting for your friend. If you are invited for dinner, you should not be more than half an hour late; for parties, nobody turns up less than an hour or an hour and a half after the time stated. You might also find that Chileans who have lived abroad are better at timekeeping.

Chileans can be very vague when agreeing to meet up. Unless you are very relaxed, the typical phrase "*Nos vemos mañana tipín las siete*" ("Let's see each other tomorrow around seven") should put you on high alert . . . especially if you're busy and can't free up time easily. Ask for more information, as the expression *tipín* (around) is too vague to be relied upon.

A NOTE ON BEHAVIOR

Chileans value good manners and are generally quite discreet. If you are invited to a party, try to meet everybody briefly before starting longer conversations with some of the guests. If you are invited to a family gathering, again talk to everybody, starting, if possible, with the older members of the family. (See pages 155–7 for greetings.) Unless you know the hosts well or the atmosphere is visibly relaxed and easygoing, be rather formal. Chileans will warm up and be very hospitable and welcoming quite quickly.

Drink with moderation, especially the surprisingly strong cocktails. Although Chileans can get merry and drink as much as any other people, explicit drunkenness is frowned upon. They like to joke about foreigners' inability to cope with their powerful and generous cocktails, but adults generally do not drink excessively. There are obvious exceptions to such moderate behavior, such as Independence Day, when the entire country lets itself go in an orgy of alcohol and food. Join in, but remember that, according to the popular media, during these festivities the average Chilean eats around 4,000 calories a day and puts on nearly 9 pounds (4 kilograms)!

If you are invited to a party in the exclusive Santiago boroughs of Lo Barnechea, La Reina, or Las Condes and you don't know the hosts very well, it is better to play it safe if you want to avoid *faux pas.* Wear something smart and discreet, and be quite careful about the conversational topics— for instance, it's a good idea to steer clear of politics. Traditional upper-class families are very fond of displaying cultivated manners, but can be quite conservative and stiff. Less well-off Chileans are much more relaxed and approachable.

Conversation

Chileans are very good at small talk and are generally socially skilled and friendly. Their sense of personal space is less defined than in many Anglo-Saxon countries, and they can be quite tactile. You may find that a new acquaintance will tap your shoulders or arms to attract your attention or reinforce a joke. Chileans are generally very proud of their country and love talking about its attractions and travel in general, although only a few can afford it. Be sensitive to your friends' economic situation when talking about your own travels or your standard of living.

Chileans tend to feel isolated and cut off from the rest of the world. You will often hear people complaining that Chile gets any new trend or product later than everybody else. People may also express frustration with the fact that Chile has a long way to go before becoming a first-world country. However justified such self-criticism might be, avoid agreeing with it and do not make any negative comments. Also avoid controversial subjects such as Pinochet, politics, and human rights issues, unless they are introduced by Chileans themselves. These are not suitable for small talk, and some Chileans might be annoyed by yet another foreigner who feels that he or she knows better. For a safe and politically correct conversation, mirror the Chileans and inquire about the family, Chilean food and geography, wines, or the economy. You may be surprised at how quickly tactfulness and trust can shift the conversation to more interesting topics.

HUMOR AND *PICARDÍA*
The Chilean sense of humor can take you by surprise. Chileans are straightfaced and

particularly enjoy "pulling your leg." Their jokes contrast subtly with their apparently reserved manner, and an inexperienced foreigner could easily be disoriented and take things at face value. Chilean jokes take advantage of an unaware victim; they are quick and unexpected, generally do not have any major consequences, and can be slightly childish. Enjoy them; with time you will realize that you can actually reciprocate without causing offense.

Another typical trait, especially among men, is sexual innuendo. Chilean slang is particularly rich in sexually loaded expressions. Some are subtle, while others are extremely vulgar. The Chileans are masters at playing with double meanings, especially with close friends, which makes it hard for foreigners to join in these types of conversations. If you find yourself in such a situation and you are among friends, don't be afraid to ask them to explain, though you may face embarrassed sniggers and a swift change of topic. Chances are that they will remind you that Chilean is the most difficult Spanish of all, very complicated and full of slang. This is not really a criticism: on the contrary, most Chileans are proud of their language, which challenges even native Spanish speakers. Your friends will disclose a world of metaphors, innuendo, and *humor criollo* (Creole humor).

FLIRTING

There is a saying among some Chilean women: "If you're depressed, go for a walk near a building site!" Workers on scaffolds are extremely free with their comments on female passersby, and Chilean women never fail to appreciate the uplifting effects of "classic *machismo*!" A Belgian friend who lives in Chile is now shocked by what she defines as the "asexuality" of Belgian streets. She feels that, although women should strive for parity and independence, a little compliment does no harm—like her shoemaker, who could not spell her name on the receipt, and decided to put "*la señora bonita*" ("the beautiful lady") instead.

In Chile, men stare at women on the street, make comments, and sometimes pay extremely romantic and "improbable" compliments. Don't be surprised if a colleague or a business partner suddenly abandons his professional image to praise your charms. There are no rules about how to react to such comments, and some women might find them irritating and sexist. Whether you ignore them or not, just remember to take these seemingly flirtatious comments in the context of a Latin American *macho* culture.

THE CHILEANS AT HOME

Daily life depends very much on class, income, and geographical area. Wealthier Chileans can afford to spend money on cultural and leisure activities, long vacations abroad, or weekend breaks on the coast. They live in comfortable houses and employ cleaners and babysitters. They also enjoy much greater job security. The lower classes live more precariously, often juggling several jobs; they sometimes live in areas with poor public services and long commutes to work. In rural areas many Chileans struggle to find permanent employment and are forced into temporary work, often as harvesters. In some very remote areas, peasants still have an old-fashioned lifestyle: they take their children to school on horseback and draw water from a well outside the home. Their daily life is very different from that of a *santiaguino*.

HOUSING

The size and style of a Chilean house will vary according to social class and geographical location.

In Santiago and other major cities, most middle-class families live in apartments, although the quality of the building and of the common parts varies greatly. Modern districts like Las Condes or La Florida have guarded multistorey blocks with gardens, garages, and many facilities. Apartments are very modern, usually on one floor, with well-proportioned rooms and a balcony. Apartment blocks located in good boroughs normally have a porter, a gardener, and sometimes a swimming pool. In the town center or other less prestigious areas, apartment blocks (often built in the 1970s) are more dated and sometimes in need of repairs, but they may be in a charming "retro" style.

In many Chilean towns, including Santiago's older boroughs, some families still live in traditional houses. Old properties from the 1930s and '40s are designed on the colonial model, with a central courtyard surrounded by the main rooms. Unfortunately, many have been demolished to make way for modern apartments. Wealthier Chileans live in large villas hidden behind high walls and leafy gardens. These villas are often quite grand and may have a tennis court, a swimming pool, a barbecue area, and other amenities. In Santiago, luxurious properties are situated in the north of the city in La Dehesa, Lo Barnechea, and La Reina. At the opposite end of the social scale, poor neighborhoods often have very basic services. Low-income homes range from small two-story detached houses, often built with state subsidies, to extremely simple rural dwellings or shacks in the capital's shantytowns.

In the Lake Region, houses are often built in a Germanic or Alpine style: they resemble Swiss cottages or German timber-framed buildings. Further south, houses were traditionally made of wood in the pioneer style. In Patagonia, wealthier homes copied early twentieth-century European architecture, and were furnished with luxurious imported furniture and fabrics. Today, the typical Patagonian home consists of a wooden structure covered by an outer metal shell and tin roof. On

the island of Chiloé traditional homes are still built with wooden tiles (*tejuelas*), which are assembled to form a beautiful herring-bone pattern. Some are brightly painted and built on stilts. As in Patagonia, high-maintenance wood is often replaced by synthetic materials or metal.

In the northern Andean areas traditional houses are built of *adobe*, a mix of straw and mud, and wealthier homes follow the traditional colonial style, enclosing a courtyard.

Chilean houses rarely have central heating and people use gas, kerosene, or sometimes electric heaters. As the heating is often concentrated in only a few rooms, winters can be quite uncomfortable. In the south, where the climate is colder, many houses still use the *cocina económica* (wood-fired kitchen stove). Even in areas as cold as Patagonia bedrooms are seldom heated. Water is heated by means of a gas boiler (*calefón*) and houses are often poorly insulated. In Chiloé some rural families still use the *fogón*, an open fire placed in a cavity in the middle of the kitchen. Wealthier homes and offices have central heating.

RENTING AN APARTMENT

Apartments for rent are usually unfurnished. In Chile, this means absolutely empty with the sole exception of the kitchen sink. Furnished apartments are more expensive, but are available at some real estate agents. Rental agreements normally last for two years, although they always include an opt-out clause with ninety days' notice. Apartment shares are common among university students. The rent or purchase price of a property can be expressed in

Chilean pesos, U.S. dollars, or UF (*Unidad de Fomento*), a peso price unit calculated daily and based on the consumer price index.

MAIDS: *PUERTA AFUERA* OR *PUERTA ADENTRO*

Middle- and upper-class households often have maids. These are colloquially called *nanas*, although strictly they are *empleadas del hogar* (domestic employees), who not only look after the children, but also cook and clean the house. Some *nanas* live with the family (in which case they are popularly known as *puerta adentro*, literally "inside the door"); others (*puerta afuera*, or "outside the door") simply stay during the day and work from Monday to Saturday. Wealthier families can employ more than one servant: they have chauffeurs, gardeners, cleaners, and babysitters. Domestic employees are seen as a sign of status, and wealthy women employ home help even when they are not working themselves, to be able to use their free time for leisure activities.

According to some, this class-conscious attitude is sometimes reflected in the bad treatment of *nanas*, who are, for example, asked to address their employers in a formal manner, but are in turn treated with disrespect. In many families, however, *nanas* become a key point of reference for the children, and everybody becomes very attached to them. Domestic employment used to be the most accessible occupation for poorer and less educated immigrants from the south, in particular for young girls of Mapuche origin. Today, most *nanas* come from Peru.

BIRTH AND CHILDHOOD

Chilean culture revolves around the family and the Catholic religion, and not surprisingly marriage and the birth of a child are among the most important events in an individual's life.

A birth is celebrated with presents and large bouquets of flowers. In Chilean hospitals, nurses normally shave the heads of newborn babies, in the belief that this will make their hair grow stronger. The baptism ceremony is followed by lunch with the family. In rural areas it is a much larger feast, which often ends with a big *asado*; guests traditionally receive a pink or pale blue sugar rose with a little baby figure on the top.

At the age of eight, children receive their First Communion and are later confirmed. Both ceremonies are key Catholic events and the child is accompanied by a *padrino* or *madrina* (godfather or godmother). In addition to birthdays, Chileans also celebrate their saint's day, usually with a family party and a cake.

EDUCATION

In Chile education is universally considered the key driver of progress, but at the same time it is a sector that leaves room for improvement. Education has been a common theme and preoccupation of different governments, and Chile's education system has gone through many radical changes, depending on the political complexion of the government of the day. The present system is largely the result of the privatizations and deregulation introduced under the Pinochet regime, although the subsequent democratic governments have carried out several reforms to make it fairer.

Compulsory education starts at the age of six, when children attend the *escuela básica*, lasting for eight years. At fourteen, they move on to the *colegio medio* until the age of eighteen. The school year runs from mid-March to mid-December, with a long summer break from around Christmas to March, and a two-week winter break in July. The school day lasts from 8:30 a.m. to 4:30 p.m., and pupils are required to wear uniforms (which closely resemble those in the U.K.).

Today, Chilean families can choose between state-run (*pública*), subsidized (*subvencionada*), and private (*privada*) schools. State-run schools are free and open to everybody. Subsidized schools are privately managed, but receive state funds; they are less expensive than private schools and have certain entry requirements. All schools follow the same curriculum and should offer the same number of weekly hours; however, while state-run schools sometimes work in shifts, the private ones all offer afternoon classes and plenty of extracurricular activities. So, although Chile has one of the highest levels of literacy in Latin America, many people complain that state-run schools have been neglected by the state and are often unable to provide a decent education. This multitiered system is considered elitist and exclusive. Private schools are often managed by the Church, in particular by the powerful Opus Dei organization and the Jesuits. As private entities, religious schools can deny admission to the children of unmarried or separated parents.

Students who want to attend university must take the PSU, or *Prueba de Selección Universitaria* (equivalent to the British A-level). This complex exam is set by the government, and admission to the best universities relies entirely on getting high grades. Students from private schools are automatically advantaged as, in addition to a higher standard of teaching, they often receive extra preuniversity training. Every year, during exam time, the country engages in a fierce debate about the unfairness of this test and the elitism of the national education system. In 2005 the famous economist Manuel Riesco denounced the fact that 70 percent of the best PSU results were gained by students from private schools, which cater to only 8 percent of the school population.

In Chile university courses normally last between five and seven years. The level of teaching is generally very good and is among the highest in Latin America. Students from low-income families can apply for a loan, which must be repaid when they find employment. Universities award a *título* (degree) and graduates are called *licenciados*. Although Chilean universities attract students from all of Latin America, many Chileans dream of studying abroad, especially in the United States. This is a privilege that only a few, mostly very wealthy, students can enjoy.

MILITARY SERVICE

The Chilean armed forces consist of four different corps: the army, the navy, the air force, and finally the *carabineros* (police). Military service (which lasts from one to two years, depending on the corps) is compulsory for all eighteen-year-old male citizens. University students can postpone it, however. Recently, women have been able to join the armed forces, although career opportunities are still very limited.

As in the rest of Latin America, the armed forces have played a very important political role throughout Chile's history. The navy and the air force were the main drivers behind the 1973 coup, and the *junta militar* ruled the country till 1989. Still today, the armed forces are a powerful political player. However, since the end of Pinochet's mandate as head of the Chilean armed forces in 1998, they have been more willing to admit to their past misconduct and undergo some reforms. The *carabineros* are highly respected. They are normally very helpful and, unlike many other developing countries, take pride in their integrity. Attempting to bribe an officer is not a good idea—it will land you in serious trouble!

MARRIAGE

Although the number of civil weddings has increased in recent years, the majority of Chileans still opt for a religious ceremony. Traditionally, couples would buy wedding rings for the engagement, have them blessed by a priest, and wear the rings on the right hand. At the wedding ceremony, the rings would be swapped from the right to the left hand. Today, few couples follow this tradition, as many have adopted the more common custom of giving the fiancée both an engagement and a wedding ring.

The format of the wedding is very similar to Catholic weddings elsewhere. There are no bridesmaids, and the bride and groom are accompanied by a *padrino* or *madrina de matrimonio* (one of the parents or a close friend). In Chile, especially among the lower classes, a wedding can easily turn into a community affair, as friends and family all participate in organizing the ceremony and the party. Among the lower classes, all guests must be invited to both the church and the meal, while upper-class families often have two guest lists—one for people who are invited to attend the entire event and one for those who are expected only at the church. *Listas de novio* (wedding lists) are becoming increasingly popular, but gift certificates are not appreciated.

WORK AND DAILY LIFE

Latin Americans generally have a long working week. In Chile a recent law has reduced the normal working week to forty-five hours (from forty-eight). People usually start work at 9:00 a.m. and finish around 6:00 p.m., Monday to Friday, but these times may vary. In addition to the official working hours, many employees in big cities have a long commute to work and don't go home for lunch, so life can be very stressful. In the provinces, life is generally slower and more relaxed. Most Chileans have a minimum of fifteen days' holiday a year, which they normally take in January and February. Unemployment benefits are extremely low and granted only for a maximum of five months.

SHOPPING AND LEISURE

In the small villages, life goes on untouched by the big retail groups. Here, people shop at small local markets and in shops that close for lunch and offer a very limited choice. On Chiloé locals still sell fruit and vegetables by the

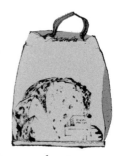

traditional measure, the *almud* (8 liters, or about 2 U.S. gal.). However, such practices are gradually disappearing, as large supermarkets, drugstore chains, and, in larger towns, malls push small trade out of business. Globalization and development have dramatically changed Chilean shopping habits. Many Chileans are proud of this change: large retailers, especially in remote areas like Patagonia, can now provide people with cheaper and better fresh produce, and bring the latest fashions from the capital and overseas. In the larger towns many Chileans spend a great proportion of their free time in malls, though it is not unusual to find vehement critics of such consumerism. This retail boom will make your stay very comfortable and safe, as you will be able to find practically everything you need, but don't miss the popular colorful fish and vegetable markets, especially in the coastal towns. In Santiago, the *galerías* in the center and the areas around Calle Patronato still retain some of their old charm.

Shops are usually open from 9:00 or 10:00 a.m. to 7:30 or 8:00 p.m. Many shops, except in large towns, close for lunch between 12:30 or 1:30 and 3:00 p.m. Large supermarkets and shopping centers are open until 10:00 p.m. and on Sundays.

HEALTH PROVISION

As with education, Chile has a two-tier health system. The public health service is accessible to everybody, but it is completely free only to the two lowest income groups. Although recent governments have done much to increase coverage, and key indicators such as child mortality have improved significantly, the national health service is often understaffed and under-equipped with long waiting lists. Public dental care, for example, can only cope with serious cases.

Better-off Chileans sign up for a private insurance scheme, ISAPRE, which gives access to a first-world standard of facilities and care. The difference between the two schemes is shocking and reveals that Chilean society is still very stratified and unequal. In 2005, however, the government of President Lagos introduced a revolutionary reform, the Plan Auge: this specifies a number of medical conditions for which private hospitals have to provide free medical assistance to the poorest citizens.

If you happen to visit a specialist, don't be surprised if he or she welcomes you with a hug and asks large numbers of questions. In Chile, a doctor is expected to be warm and to devote lots of attention to the patient. With regular visits he or she will almost treat you like an old friend. Such experiences, however, are likely to be confined to the private health system; in the overstretched state-run sector, things are very different.

chapter six

TIME OUT

As we have seen, Chilean social life revolves around the family. On Sunday, for example, the majority of Chileans gather at their parents' house for lunch. Families often eat together in the evenings. Friends tend to meet at home, and visits to relatives can often be spontaneous, with no advance calls. Families tend to do things together even when the children are older. Chileans like to meet in the center of town in the late afternoon for a stroll, an ice cream, or an aperitif. In the evening, many go out for a drink or, in cities, to the cinema and theater. Activities vary depending on the city and social class. Upper-class women who do not work spend time at the tennis club, play bridge, or go to the gym. Those with little home help tend to be very busy juggling their job, looking after the children, and doing the housework. On Saturday they often end up shopping, cleaning, and cooking the family lunch. Chileans love football, but are generally not very sporty. They like being outdoors, but more to enjoy a barbecue than a strenuous hike.

EATING AND DRINKING

Food plays a pivotal role in Chilean social life.
Families and friends often meet for a meal at
home, and traditional festivities are celebrated
with huge feasts of meat or seafood.
Chilean cuisine is generally not very
elaborate, makes good use of the fresh
produce of land and sea, and reflects
the cultural and ethnic makeup of the
country. Each region has its own
specialties, although there are some
national dishes and snacks that can be
found across the country.

Most Chileans have a sweet tooth and love red
meat. They prefer sparkling water to still or spring
water, although at home you would seldom be
served water with your meal, as many Chileans
prefer to offer soft drinks or juices made with
flavored powders. The trend toward healthy food
is only just starting, and is confined to the
wealthiest families living in the main cities. Fast-
food joints, in both American and Chilean style,
are invading the cities and offer a variety of
hyper-calorific snacks. The southern regions have
the most amazing variety of seafood: mussels,
clams, scallops, and many other species you may
never even have heard of, simply steamed and
served with a spicy sauce or cooked in hearty
soups. All savory dishes are served with lemons

cut in half and placed on the table. Lemon juice may be added to all seafood, soups, and salads. Chileans usually eat the main dish with rice, or potatoes, while bread is served before the starter with butter or *pebre*, a typical sauce made of diced onions, tomatoes, peppers, coriander, and spicy *ají* (chili). *Pebre* is a ubiquitous sauce, used especially with grilled meat. Finally, no Chilean meal would be complete without enjoying the national aperitifs, *pisco* sour and *vaina* (see below), and several glasses of wine.

Meal Times

Breakfast is generally very light, consisting of coffee with milk or tea and fresh bread or *tostadas* (toasts) with jam and butter. Hotels and bed-and-breakfast establishments might serve scrambled eggs, but these are rarely eaten in Chilean homes.

Lunch is traditionally the main meal of the day, although this is gradually changing, especially in the large cities, as people tend to have shorter lunch breaks and most schools provide lunch. It is eaten between 1:00 and 3:00 p.m., and can range from a large traditional meal (at home or in a restaurant) to a snack.

Dinner starts around 8:30 to 9:00 p.m., but in summer it tends to be much later. Families will eat a larger evening meal if they have not had a proper lunch.

A Note on Coffee and Tea

Chile has not developed a strong coffee culture. Apart from specialist cafés and good-quality restaurants, which offer *corto* (espresso) or *cortado* (a small cappuccino), coffee is typically made with instant coffee granules or with filters. The Chilean version of cappuccino is coffee with whipped cream on top.

Unless specified otherwise, tea is drunk black and seldom served in a pot. British visitors may be horrified to find that *té con leche* (tea with milk) is often a tea bag dunked in a cup of hot milk. If you don't want black tea, ask specifically for a slice of lemon or cold milk. There is a wide variety of herbal teas, including camomile (*manzanilla*), typically drunk as a *bajativo* (digestive).

Once

Once (pronounced "on-say", and literally meaning "eleven") is a unique Chilean creation, a mix between the traditional Spanish *merienda* (light afternoon snack) and English afternoon tea. The origin of the name *once* is still debated, and there are many explanations. According to the most curious one, *once* was the name that workers used for the *aguardiente* (a strong spirit) they used to drink secretly during their breaks. To hide this practice, they named it after the number of letters in the word *aguardiente*!

Once is taken between 4:00 and 8:00 p.m. and includes tea or coffee, warm bread with jam, butter, ham, cheese, avocado, and tomato. In Region X (the Lake Region) the German immigrants have created a richer version of this Chilean snack, the *once alemana* (meaning "German *once*"), which includes cakes and various pâtés.

Traditional Specialties
It is impossible to do justice to the richness and variety of Chilean food in a few words. As in many other Latin American countries, the cuisine is the result of the encounter between indigenous and European culinary traditions.

The most traditional dishes are hearty and made of the simplest local ingredients. *Pastel de choclo* is a sweet corn and meat pie. The typical large Chilean corn (*choclo*) is also used to prepare the *humita*, an ancient pre-Columbian dish. The corn is mashed and mixed with onions and basil, wrapped in the cob leaves, and steamed. Perhaps the most original dish is the *curanto*, a feast of shellfish and meat that is eaten on the island of Chiloé. *Curanto*, which means "place of stone" in the Mapuche language, Mapudungun, is traditionally prepared by a family to thank friends and neighbors for their help in a major undertaking, like sowing or harvesting the crops.

Layers of shellfish, meat, sausages, potatoes, and local potato bread are placed in a hole in the ground over some charcoal covered by stones. Each layer is separated by leaves of the *pangue*, or giant rhubarb. Visitors will hardly ever be offered the traditional *curanto*, however (though large groups of tourists can order it in advance). What is usually served nowadays is a "domesticated" version called *pullmay* or *curanto en olla* ("*curanto* in the pot"), which is simply cooked on a stove.

Meat

Chileans love grilled meat. *Parrilladas* and *asados* are the favorites at festivities and gatherings. A *parrillada* consists of a generous portion of different meat cuts with *prieta* (a blood sausage), *longanizas* (traditional sausages), and potatoes. The name refers to the *parrilla*, the hot grill plate with charcoal, which is brought to the table together with *pebre*, and

salads. *Carne asada* is the generic term for grilled meat. As we have seen, Chileans often organize an *asado* on weekends or in the summer. In southern Chile, people prefer *asado de cordero* (lamb barbecue), which can be grilled on a *parrilla*, but most typically on a skewer (*al palo*).

Asado al palo is generally found in the more rural areas of the south, and is one of the main Patagonian dishes. It is the ultimate experience for any carnivore, and a vegetarian's worst nightmare, as it consists of a whole skinned lamb impaled on a huge cross-shaped skewer. The skewer is placed vertically next to a large wooden fire or horizontally over it. The cooking process is much slower than in a *parrillada,* giving a deliciously buttery consistency to the meat.

"Meaty" Terminology

In addition to the *parrillada* and *asado al palo,* some restaurants (usually called *asadores*) offer a wide variety of individual meat cuts, cooked to the customer's taste. When taking an order, the waiter will always ask, "*Cómo quiere la carne?*" ("How would you like your meat done?"). Chileans have several terms to indicate the degree of cooking; the following are the most common across the entire country.

Bleu/A punto/Inglesa Very rare	
Medio Medium rare	
Tres cuartos Almost done, just slightly rare in the middle	
Bien hecha Well done	

The above applies only to beef. All other meat is served well done.

Lomo a lo pobre is one of the most popular Chilean dishes. This is a hyper-calorific and at times greasy dish consisting of a large steak accompanied by fried onions, fried eggs, french fries, and boiled rice!

Seafood

Chile is a paradise for seafood lovers. The country is blessed with one of the richest seas in the world and has a tradition of delicious recipes, sometimes using the oddest sea creatures. Although seafood is eaten throughout the country, the tastiest varieties are found in the southern regions, from Chiloé to Patagonia. *Caldillos*, *pailas*, and *cazuelas* are all broths or chowders with various shellfish and other ingredients. They are so tasty and so typically southern Chilean that Pablo Neruda celebrated them in his *Oda al caldillo de Congrio* ("Ode to the Conger Eel Chowder")! *Chupes* are thick and creamy gratin dishes, generally made with shellfish or *centolla*, a large crab. Crab (*jaiba*) and abalone (*loco*) are the top delicacies of the south. They are generally steamed and simply served without the shell with mayonnaise and lemon.

Empanadas

The king of Chilean snacks is undoubtedly the *empanada*, a half-moon-shaped pie of bread dough or, less frequently, puff pastry, with a variety of fillings. *Empanadas* can be baked or fried, are sold in bakeries, bars, and supermarkets, and are served as nibbles in some restaurants. Although *empanadas* are eaten throughout South America, Chile has some of the widest choice of fillings. The *empanada de pino* is the most typically Chilean; it is oven baked and filled with onions, meat, hard-boiled eggs, sultanas, and olives. Small fried *empanadas* and *pebre* are the typical accompaniment to a *pisco* sour as an aperitif.

Sweets

Chile has a large variety of sweets, but surprisingly only a limited range is eaten at meals or offered as dessert in restaurants. The dessert menu always includes fruit salad and several cream or ice-cream based desserts. The most original Chilean dessert is *mote con huesillo*, a thirst-quenching and nutritious drink made of boiled dry peaches and toasted wheat. It can sometimes be found in restaurants, but is more typically sold at street kiosks in busy city areas or parks.

Drinks

Chileans are very proud of their wines, although widespread consumption and appreciation is a relatively recent phenomenon. For years, only the upper class could afford good wines, while the rest of the population, especially in the rural areas, used to mix wine with juice, or drink *chicha* (fizzy fermented grape juice). Today, Chileans have learned to appreciate their wines. They have a great choice of white, red, and sparkling wines that use most international grape varieties such as Merlot and Chardonnay, and the rare Carmenère. In the countryside, and in particular for traditional festivities, people drink *chicha* or *chicha de manzana* (cider). Beer is widely drunk, especially by young people.

Pisco is the most popular strong spirit. It is used to prepare the main national cocktails: *vaina*, where it is mixed with port, cognac, egg yolks, and chocolate; and *pisco* sour, with lemon juice, egg white, and sugar. *Piscola* is *pisco* with Coca Cola. At Christmas Chileans drink *cola de mono* (literally, "monkey's tail"), a delicious mix of *aguardiente*, spices, coffee, and condensed milk, sometimes called the poor man's Bailey's.

EATING OUT

Although Chileans have a passion for food, they tend to eat at home, and go out to restaurants only on special occasions. There is a wide variety of options for both snacks and proper meals. Although food is becoming increasingly multicultural, international cuisine is restricted to the main cities, where Peruvian, Italian, and oriental are the most frequent "exotic" options. Bars and the ubiquitous *fuente de sodas* (bar with no alcohol license) are ideal for a light snack. They are open all day and serve food at the bar or at the table. Equally cheap and easy are the *cocinerías* or *comedores* (found in markets), which serve typical Chilean food till around 9:00 p.m. Except for the *Mercado Central* (central market) in Santiago, *cocinerías* are generally patronized by locals, and tourists are not hassled.

Restaurants are pricier and more formal. They tend to open from 1:00 to 3:00 p.m. and again from 7:30 p.m. to 12:00 or 1:00 a.m., but Chileans usually start dining between 9:30 and 10:00 p.m. Before 9:30 p.m. you are likely to be on your own or with other foreigners. It's not unusual to see Chileans entering a restaurant at 11:30 p.m., although most reservations are made for between 9:30 and 10:00 p.m. Most restaurants close around midnight to 1:00 a.m., but will serve latecomers.

Service is normally quite slow and there are no dedicated non-smoking areas. Credit cards are widely accepted, though smaller establishments and bars normally take cash only.

> ### *TIPPING*
> A minimum 10 percent tip is recommended in restaurants and pubs. Leave the tip on the table and avoid adding it to the credit card payment—this is to ensure that it reaches the waiter or waitress. Taxi drivers do not usually expect a tip unless they help you with the luggage. Tip the porter in hotels (minimum 500 pesos).

ENTERTAINMENT

During the week people meet up right after work. They join colleagues or meet friends around 6:30–7:00 p.m. for a beer or an aperitif. Although one cannot generalize, the higher social classes tend to have a more restrained and exclusive social life after work. The lower and middle classes meet at bars and drink *piscola* or beer, often served in pitchers. Foreign spirits, like whiskey, are more expensive and are sometimes considered classier. In the countryside, such gatherings generally exclude women and the drinking can get quite heavy. In towns, social divides become visible through the choice of venue and in some cases the amount of alcohol consumed, although it is quite rare to witness displays of drunkenness.

Nightlife

Nightlife (known as *carrete*) starts very late. Chileans usually have dinner at home before going out. Younger people will gather at a friend's house before venturing out to the bars around 10:00 or 10.30 p.m., or even later. The main cities have a wide range of bars and discos. Pubs are normally quite intimate and people tend to sit at the table and rarely stand. Smoking is still fashionable, in particular among women.

Some pubs put on jazz concerts; others, also called disco-pubs, have a dance floor and live music. The public participates and cheers the

singer, but there is little intermingling between groups sitting at different tables. Dancing starts around 1:30 a.m. and so do the discos, which close around 5:00 a.m. The music varies according to the type of venue.

The more working-class and rural establishments, especially in the south, play *ranchera* (country music). Chileans tend to dance in couples even when they are in groups. Women will go out in groups and dance together. Chileans love dancing, as we have seen, but they are much less exuberant than other Latin Americans.

Discos often compete by advertising the length of their bar and the size of their dance floor. The cover charge includes one drink, usually a *piscola*, a beer, or a soft drink. Some discos don't charge women between 10:00 and 12:00 p.m. Others have a *viernes femenino* (women's Friday), an early show including male dancers. The dress code varies with the style of the venue, but Chileans are generally quite relaxed and casual. In Santiago, try the bohemian borough Barrio Bellavista, which has a wide range of pubs, discos, and restaurants. Dress up and venture out to El Bosque and the Paseo de San Damián for more upper-class options.

Cinema and Theater

Chileans enjoy going to the cinema and the theater, although the choice tends to be limited in the smaller towns. The main cities have a variety of venues and organize summer festivals. Santiago, for example, has a great choice of cinemas, including commercial multiscreen centers, mainly in malls in the northern districts, and some art-house cinemas that show European films or host themed festivals. Blockbusters are generally dubbed, while less commercial films are subtitled. In the provinces, everything arrives with a time delay according to the distance from the capital.

The capital and the main university towns have a vibrant cultural scene, in particular for fringe theater. Music and theater performances of  all kind usually start around 8:30 p.m. and are very popular. The public is mixed and prices are quite affordable. Since the return to democracy, new Chilean talents have emerged to enliven the cultural life of the cities. The major events take place in the warm season. In January Santiago hosts a series of interesting events, such as *Santiago a Mil*, an international fringe theater festival, and other prestigious performances.

OUTDOOR ACTIVITIES

For many foreigners, Chile is a paradise of natural beauty and outdoor activities. Surprisingly, Chileans take relatively little advantage of the nature around them. Although there are increasing numbers who go trekking in parks and engage in other outdoor activities, the average Chilean is rather sedentary, enjoying his or her comforts and not seeing the point of getting tired and sweaty on a long walk! Chileans often prefer to drive out into the countryside, have a barbecue with friends and family, and relax with a bottle of wine in the shade. Don't be misled if you are invited *al campo* (to the countryside). Remember that some outdoor activities like skiing, surfing, or trekking in the south are still very expensive for the average Chilean family.

Football is by far the most popular sport in Chile and is played at all levels, from school to the professional clubs. There are thousands of football teams that represent towns, universities, and even national minorities like Unión Española or the Green Cross de los Palestinos. The most famous teams are Colo Colo, Universidad de Chile, and Universidad Católica. Gyms are not as popular in Chile as in the U.S.A. Tennis is played by the middle and upper classes, and Marcelo Ríos made history as the first Latin American to reach number one in ATP world rankings in 1998. Horse racing is another national passion. Though only the upper class can actually afford to go riding, betting and watching horse racing are enjoyed by all classes. Golf is still an extremely exclusive sport, which is confined to the business elite. Basketball is commonly played in the south.

In the central and southern regions, in particular around the town of Rancagua, Chileans still maintain the tradition of *rodeos chilenos,* which take place especially in March. The Chilean rodeo involves two men on horseback trying to immobilize a bull against the wall of the arena.

MONEY AND BANKING

The Chilean currency is the *peso chileno* (Chilean peso) and, somewhat confusingly, it uses the U.S. dollar sign ($). It is used in all transactions and you should not be misled by some tourist establishments trying to sell you services in U.S. dollars (especially excursions). Always ask for prices in Chilean currency as they are often cheaper.

ATMs are widely available in Chile and are the safest option. (Note that they are blocked on election days, so remember to withdraw cash beforehand.) Cirrus and PLUS cards are accepted by almost all ATMs, but remember that the smaller towns often do not have any banking facilities, so try to withdraw cash in provincial and major towns. Banks are open from 9:00 a.m. to 2:00 p.m.

Credit cards are accepted in most hotels, restaurants, large shops, and even bus stations, but you will need cash for small guest houses, bars, and other purchases. No surcharge should be applied when paying by credit card, but you will always be asked to write down your passport number (*número de cédula*). If you don't want to take your passport with you, just learn the number by heart, as nobody will actually demand to see the document before accepting payment. Dollars are not generally accepted, but can be changed in hotels or *casas de cambio* (bureaux de change). Traveler's checks are very safe, but are probably unnecessary if you have a credit and debit card.

chapter seven

TRAVEL, HEALTH, & SAFETY

FLYING

Customs and visa procedures on arrival are quite efficient. Chile's main cities are well connected by a network of flights operated mainly by the national airline, LanChile. Once in Chile foreigners are charged very high prices, so the cheapest way to fly internally is to buy a flight pass before arriving in the country. Passes for domestic flights are issued by LanChile, Iberia, and the One World Alliance; there are also passes that are valid across several countries in Latin America. Passes must be purchased in association with an international air ticket and include a minimum of three internal flights.

Domestic fights are generally on time and the service is impeccable. Ask for a seat on the left if you are flying southward and on the right if you are flying north: on a clear day you will be able to see the Andes and its glaciers. Keep your luggage receipts as these may be checked when leaving the terminal. There is no departure tax, so you can spend your pesos before leaving for the airport.

TRAINS

Chile's railway network was built during the nineteenth and early twentieth centuries. Railways were widely used until the late 1960s and '70s, but lack of investment and a preference for road transportation mean that most lines are no longer in use. A few lines still operate in the center and the north. There are three classes of fare: *economía*, *salón*, and *cama* (simple sleeping facilities). Trains are generally cheap, but slower and less frequent than buses.

BY SEA

Sailing is one of the best ways to view the beauty of the coast. The most spectacular routes are in the south, particularly to Chiloé and in Patagonia. The island of Chiloé is connected to the mainland by a series of ferries (*barcos*) leaving in the north from near Puerto Montt and in the south from Quellón. Southern Patagonia has the most expensive options: the *Navimag* leaves Puerto Natales for a three-day journey to Puerto Montt, and other operators offer transport to Isla Navarino. When traveling by sea, be sure to take very warm clothes and sea sickness tablets. The Golfo de Penas (Bay of Sorrows) is one of the most turbulent stretches of the Pacific.

BUSES

Buses are ideal for short trips. Given the length of the country, long-distance travel by bus would entail many hours on the road and overnight journeys. Although the main roads are paved, rural destinations are often linked by bumpy dirt roads, and journeys on bone-rattling buses can be uncomfortable, slow, and very dusty, so it is worth combining short bus trips with internal flights.

The quality of buses has improved greatly. They are generally on time, never overcrowded, and usually have assigned seats. Although most towns have a bus station (*terminal de buses*), bus companies are sometimes scattered around town, so always check the address first. At border crossings, everybody has to get off the bus with their passport and hand luggage. Procedures are easygoing although not always swift, and you might be searched. It is forbidden to bring fresh unpacked food, fruit, and vegetables into Chile. If found, these will almost certainly be confiscated.

URBAN TRANSPORTION

The most commonly used forms of urban transportation are *micros* and *colectivos*. *Micros* are usually large buses, or less frequently minivans. They are cheap, noisy, and crowded at rush hour. They only stop at designated bus stops and never on demand in the road. Passengers get on at the front (*entrada*) and buy their ticket from the driver. In Santiago *micros* are the only public service available through the night. They cover the entire metropolitan area except for some very wealthy districts. There is no official map of the bus routes. For general inquiries, ask the tourist office; for more specific itineraries, it is better to ask directly at the bus stop or get help from the locals. Alternatively, try the amateur Web site http://www.micros.cl/.

Colectivos are shared taxis that cover a specific itinerary and can take up to four passengers. The fixed fare is usually slightly higher than on a bus, but much cheaper than ordinary taxis. They stop anywhere along their route, which is displayed on a board on the roof. The only way to find the right *colectivo* is to ask around or stop one heading in your direction and check how far it is going.

Ordinary taxis can be stopped in the street or hired at taxi stands. They normally use a meter, although in smaller towns they might charge a fixed fare. Generally there is no need to tip.

Santiago also has a very modern subway network (*metro*), which has recently been

expanded. It is generally clean and tidy, and trains
run very frequently from 6:30 a.m. to 10:30 p.m.
on weekdays and from 8:30 a.m. to 10:30 p.m. on
Sundays and bank holidays. Tickets (*boletos*) are
sold at the counter (*boletería*), at ticket machines,
and, at rush hour, by subway staff around the

station. There are
no day passes or
books of tickets.
In a way, the
metro de Santiago
symbolizes the
Chilean aspiration
for progress and
development. Some stations even provide a
wireless hot spot (*punto wireless*), and since 1996
the network has had the *Bibliómetro*, a library
service for *metro* travelers.

DRIVING

Chileans generally drive carefully and calmly. In
the main cities, particularly in Santiago, drivers
can get a bit stressed and aggressive, especially
during the rush hour, but traffic rarely reaches the
level of confusion and speed typical of other Latin
American cities. Perhaps the most dangerous
vehicles in Santiago are the *micros*. It is advisable
to keep as far away as possible from these buses,

which change lane unexpectedly and travel at very high speed, braking at the very last minute. Outside the main centers Chileans drive slowly, tend to respect the speed limits, and stop at pedestrian crossings (*cruces peatonales*). They also like honking with contempt at anybody who tries to break the rules or undertakes a reckless maneuver. Despite the record of good road behavior, drunk driving is the major cause of accidents, particularly during festivities.

Seat belts must be worn by the driver and the passenger in the front seat. Unless otherwise specified, the speed limits are 37 mph (60 kmph) in cities, 62 mph (100 kmph) outside urban areas, and 74 mph (120 kmph) on the expressways (*autopistas*). Major roads are in fairly good condition, while in the provinces roads are often unpaved. These are called *camino de ripio* (gravel) or *tierra* (literally, soil). Their condition varies greatly depending on the weather. Even paved roads can have huge potholes, so always slow down when you see the sign *Bache* (Pothole). There are only a few expressways, mainly in the Santiago area and as part of the Panamericana, the main road that runs the length of the country down to Puerto Montt. For most of them you will be required to pay a toll (*peaje*) at the exit, although this is not always clearly indicated. When driving on main roads, be warned that the signs for a turnoff may come at the very last minute, sometimes just opposite the exit itself.

In cities, the roads are usually based on a one-way system. The direction of the traffic flow is indicated by a little arrow placed under the name of the street. When driving, watch out for the signs *Pare* (Stop) and *Ceda* (Give way), and always stop at a pedestrian crossing. The road signs can be confusing. Traffic lights are sometimes placed after rather than before the junction. Also, when approaching a junction, look carefully for the one-way arrow on both sides of the road you wish to turn into, in case it has been placed only on one side of the road ahead. Look out for the *No entrar* (No entry) sign.

In Santiago, in some downtown roads the direction of traffic flow changes during the day to ease congestion. There are also antipollution measures, such as restricting the admission of cars according to odd or even registration numbers. These are regularly enforced, especially in winter.

Car Rental
Car rental is available in all major towns and at all airports. Information can be found on the Web sites of the international rental firms as well as a plethora of local companies, sometimes offering better deals (but beware of quality). If you are

traveling in the high season, book well in advance. Always check that the cost of the vehicle includes taxes. When traveling on unpaved roads (especially along the Carretera Austral in the south), 4 x 4s and pickups are recommended, although these are more expensive and not always available. Although, strictly speaking, Chilean law requires foreigners to hold an international driver's license, a valid foreign driver's license (*carnet de conducir*) is normally accepted. Some visitors on longer stays find it cheaper to purchase a car, although you will need to obtain a RUT (tax code) from the Chilean tax office.

Parking

Parking in urban areas is seldom free. There are no obvious signs showing where parking is metered, so look for the parking attendant (*aparcador*) before leaving the parking slot, otherwise you might receive a fine. In the main towns, *aparcadores* carry a portable electronic device into which they input the license plate number and the time of arrival. In smaller towns they carry a small pouch on a belt and are sometimes in uniform. They leave a receipt on the windshield and charge the driver on departure. Don't be misled by their informal appearance and the sometimes grubby piece of paper on your windshield: they are legally authorized.

At night, particularly in areas where there is nightlife, parking can be haphazard. There are often unofficial *aparcadores* who charge a tip for guiding you to the right spot or for looking after the car. Many restaurants and discos have customer parking; always tip the attendant.

The big cities also have secure parking garages, often underground. Check the opening times and remember that you may need the ticket issued at the entrance to get back into the garage. The sign for parking is "E" (*Estacionamento*), not "P."

WHERE TO STAY

There is a wide choice of accommodation, from five-star hotels to campsites or rooms in private homes. There are several words for budget and medium-range establishments, and it is not always clear what the difference is. *Hospedaje*, *residencial*, *casa de familia*, and *hostal* are the most basic. They vary in quality, from a shabby place to rooms in a family home, often with cooking facilities, and a shared bathroom. However, these terms might equally mean a guest house with a breakfast area and run like a family hotel.

Choose the simplest options if you want to get to know Chileans. Accommodation in a private home can be pleasant and intimate, particularly in the south. Establishments are usually managed by a woman, and you might even get homemade bread for breakfast, and spend the evening in the family's sitting room. The rise in backpacker tourism has attracted more commercially aware tourist operators from Santiago offering trendier equivalent accommodation, forcing these family concerns out of business. Such places may be ideal for meeting other tourists, but you will miss out on the Chilean way of life. They are, of course, an easier option if you do not speak Spanish. Simple accommodation rarely includes a private bathroom; if this is a priority, check out the *hoteles*, which are generally more expensive but not necessarily more luxurious. If you opt for mid-range accommodation, check the room and the shared facilities first. If traveling in the south, bring warm sleeping clothes as rooms do not normally have central heating.

The word *hostería* normally indicates a stylish hotel. This and the three- to five-star hotels are recommended if you are looking for comfort. Nevertheless, the standard is lower in the large cities than in the provinces. In Santiago, for example, many three-star hotels in the old town are located in beautiful colonial palaces but are run-down. Regrettably, Santiago seems to lack the well-appointed, charming colonial-style hotels often found in other Latin American cities. Tourists looking for real comfort should head for the modern Americanized hotels in the richer districts of Providencia and Las Condes. All except the simplest establishments accept credit cards. Remember that in top to mid-range hotels tipping is expected (minimum 500 pesos).

Cabañas, found in vacation resorts popular with Chilean families, are self-catering huts and bungalows. They vary in size and shape but always include a bathroom, a kitchen, and a barbecue area. They are usually booked up in February, especially in the coastal resorts around Viña del Mar and La Serena and in the Lake Region.

HEALTH

Chile does not present greater health hazards than any other country. Tap water is safe to drink in Santiago and the other main cities, but it is probably better to stick to bottled water for your initial period of stay and in all rural areas.

Chilean towns are dotted with drugstores (*farmácias*), usually part of a chain, selling everything from drugs to baby food and snacks. The staff are invariably helpful and most Western medicines are available, although at a higher price. Travel insurance is recommended.

Chile's hygiene and public health standards are among the highest in Latin America. In 1991 a cholera epidemic struck Peru and northern Chile, and people are now very aware of the need to eat only cooked seafood and to wash vegetables thoroughly. Since the outbreak, restaurants have not been allowed to serve raw seafood.

Despite the strict measures, eating seafood is always risky. Use your common sense when choosing a restaurant. Always go for the busiest place and avoid eating seafood or rare meat if you are uncertain about the establishment. If in doubt, ask the locals: they will often give excellent recommendations. If invited into a Chilean home, do not be afraid to ask for cooked seafood only.

Sun, Hypothermia, and Altitude Sickness

When visiting the south, remember that in some areas of Patagonia ultraviolet radiation is extremely high due to the thinning of the ozone layer. Use high-factor sun protection. All outdoor enthusiasts should plan their excursions carefully and bring adequate clothing. In the north, the desert region of Atacama is hot during the day and cold at night, with the risk of both heat exhaustion and hypothermia. Drink plenty of water and wear layers of clothes.

When venturing into the higher Andean areas, in particular above 9,000 feet (3,000 m), be careful of *soroche* or *apunamiento* (altitude sickness). This can cause nausea, headaches, insomnia, and shortness of breath, but most people adapt after a few days. Take it easy, breathe slowly, avoid strenuous activities, and eat light local food. Drink *mate de coca* (tea made of coca leaves) where available, avoid alcohol, and keep warm.

MAIN TOURIST ATTRACTIONS
Santiago de Chile

The capital Santiago is a must for anyone seeking

to understand Chile's past and its more recent history. It has the best museums and collections of Chilean art. Recent events have left a deep mark on the city and visitors can explore the most dramatic moments of this troubled country by visiting the Museo de la Solidaridad Salvador Allende, the presidential palace La Moneda, and the Museo de Arte Contemporaneo.

Santiago is Chile's economic center; one-third of the population live here, including a growing minority of Peruvians, Bolivians, and other Latin

Americans who have come in search of a better life. It is a city of contrasts, where modern districts flourish next to old and sometimes run-down areas, where the rich enjoy a secluded life in the leafy northern suburbs, while the less fortunate live in dusty and cold *poblaciones* (slums). However, you will not find the extremes of poverty, informality, and opulence typical of other large cities on the continent. In Santiago you can see the transformation of Chilean society, and enjoy a dynamic cultural scene. Still, this is only a partial view of the country. If you have the time, leave the capital and explore.

It is impossible to list all Chile's numerous attractions, as each region has its own charm and unique character. Here are a few selected areas.

Valparaíso

Travel north of Santiago to beautiful Valparaíso, "the pearl of the Pacific," Chile's main commercial port. Valparaíso was founded in colonial times, but became important after independence and in particular toward the end of the nineteenth century, before the opening of the Panama Canal, when it enjoyed wealth and fame thanks to its key position along the sea route from Europe to California. The most distinctive areas of the city are perched on hills, connected to sea level by beautiful *ascensores* (funicular railways).

The North

North of Valparaíso, the town of La Serena is a pleasant colonial city. Further north lies the Atacama Desert, which stretches for thousands of miles up to the Peruvian border. A few hours inland from the coast you can visit picturesque colonial villages such as San Pedro de Atacama, and experience the surreal, lunar landscape of volcanoes, desert valleys, and breathtaking high-altitude Andean lakes.

The South

Most people travel to the remote regions of southern Chile to explore its natural beauty. Pucón is the main base for climbing and white-water rafting. Further south, the landscape becomes almost Alpine, with lakes surrounded by snowy volcanoes. For an insight into the complex history of this area, visit the main cities of Temuco, Valdivia, or Puerto Montt.

Chiloé's traditional dances and music are among

the highest examples of Chilean folklore. The island is famous for its wooden churches, which were declared a UNESCO World Heritage site in 2000. *Chilote* architecture originates from the meeting of two cultures, the autochthonous wood-carving tradition and the late baroque art of the *misiones* (religious missions).

Patagonia and Easter Island

The Carretera Austral crosses part of Region XI (Aisén), a relatively unexplored area with fjords, windswept snowy peaks, and magnificent lakes. Further south, separated by a large glacier (Campo de Hielo Sur), lies Region XII, which includes Tierra del Fuego and southern Patagonia. This region has many parks, including the world-famous Torres del Paine.

A long flight away lies Easter Island, with its Polynesian traditions and the mysterious *moai*, huge stone statues scattered across the island.

Tourist locations are best avoided during the peak season from mid-January to the end of February. Wherever you go, people will be helpful and polite. Southern Chileans, in particular, are known for their hospitality and kindness.

chapter eight

BUSINESS BRIEFING

Copper, salmon, timber, wine, and fruit are just some of Chile's principal exports. Except for copper, these are all so-called "nontraditional exports," and have been promoted since the 1980s and '90s as part of the neoliberal opening up of the national economy. Although copper is still the main revenue generator, nontraditional exports and services have seen a boom due to foreign investment and to increased demand from Asia, especially China and Japan.

Since the radical economic shake-up introduced by Pinochet's Chicago Boys (see page 34), Chileans have been forced to adapt to a fast-moving economy. The 1980s saw the rise of the "Chilean yuppies," young professionals and entrepreneurs who profited from the increased demand in services, especially within the financial sector. The focus on free-market policies and foreign investment remained unchanged following the return to democracy and brought spectacular growth during the '90s. Today Chile's economy is modern and vibrant; it is geared to international trade relations, and is also increasingly expert in working with foreign investors on complex projects.

THE BUSINESS CULTURE

Changes in Chilean business mirror the general transformation of the country. Many companies are becoming less hierarchical; managers are younger than in the past, and the number of women in managerial positions is on the increase. Modern technology has largely replaced traditional practices: e-mails are widely used, and so are PowerPoint presentations and online services. Many businesspeople have embraced international values and practices, such as flexibility, efficiency, quality, and reliability; those in larger companies, especially subsidiaries of international groups, take pride in the way they have adopted a U.S.-style business culture.

For these reasons, foreigners generally find Chileans relatively easy to do business with. At least at first glance, they are not dissimilar to experienced businesspeople in Europe or the U.S.A. They are generally reliable, and usually respect agreements and deadlines; many are used to working with foreigners or have been educated at foreign business schools. The picture can be quite different for smaller companies in the provinces, however, as these businesses are not used to competition or to operating on a larger scale beyond their local or national remit.

MODERNITY AND TRADITION

Chileans generally admire professionalism and clarity, and tend to be efficient and reliable. They are eager to distance themselves from the negative stereotypes of Latin American corruption, slowness, and unreliability. Still, business practices are not entirely free from the traditional Latin culture of connections and hierarchy. The way tradition and modernity come together depends on many factors, in particular management age and education, the company's geographical location, and the industry sector.

Top managers from multinationals or large Chilean companies attend business schools in the U.S.A. or the U.K., and are firm advocates of the market economy. Their behavior is much like that of businesspeople from the U.S.A. The older generation of entrepreneurs, however, mixes a strong pro-market stance with traditional values, involving hierarchy, nepotism, and paternalism. Though they surround themselves with younger, ambitious staff, they are wedded to the old ways. Networking, respect for status and hierarchy, and impeccable style are key when dealing with them.

SANTIAGO AND THE PROVINCES

Chilean business consists of two different and completely separate worlds: Santiago and the provinces. Santiago hosts the headquarters of all important Chilean enterprises, often located in smart modern offices in the upmarket areas of the city. Their employees adopt modern practices, often speak fluent English, and may sometimes be foreign nationals.

Business in the provinces, on the other hand, is dominated by small and medium-sized firms. Their owners are generally not used to dealing with foreigners and may be very cautious—mainly because they feel their ideas could be "stolen" or they could be overpowered by stronger foreign companies. Chilean businesses have fallen prey to foreign investors in the past, in particular in the timber and fish-farming sectors. For this reason, it is important for a foreigner to build trust through open and transparent discussion. Present your bona fides and state your intentions very clearly. Once negotiations are under way, however, you may find that the initial caution is replaced by overenthusiasm. In some cases, especially when the Chileans see the opportunities of international expansion, their keenness to do business might result in improvisation and promising what they cannot deliver.

Such is the dominance of Santiago that even the major mining companies, which are based in northern Chile, centralize the decision-making process in the capital. So, unless a foreign businessperson is after a niche market or a local provider, he or she will rarely hold a meeting in the provinces.

HIERARCHY

Despite the recent changes, Chilean business has some very traditional traits. Most companies are hierarchical and old-fashioned in their treatment of staff. Although many top managers now read and write their own e-mails, many, even the youngest, have a personal assistant, normally a woman. She usually addresses her boss with the formal "you" (*usted*) and will use the respectful "*Don*" before his name (see more on pages 145 and 156–7). She sits outside his office, like a personal guard, and acts as a filter for visitors and callers. The boss normally asks her to dial phone numbers on his behalf.

In the office the lowest position is that of the "*junior*," a factotum who carries out a variety of tasks, including deliveries. The hierarchy within a company usually reflects Chilean class divisions and determines how colleagues socialize. Junior staff hardly ever mingle with senior managers. In a bank, for example, back office staff will go out for a drink after work, while senior executives organize dinners or visit each other at home. Still, colleagues are very friendly to each other and often address each other with *tú* (the informal "you"). Before Christmas and at the *Fiestas Patrias*, companies organize a party that is open to employees' families and includes an *asado* and sometimes dancing.

PITUTOS AND CHAQUETEO

Another traditional aspect of business is the importance of contacts or connections (*pitutos*). Individual career prospects are often dependent on connections and social class. Employers prefer to hire someone who has been recommended by a friend or who has a prestigious surname. A young Chilean entrepreneur who manages his own company candidly admitted that the right connections can open doors, and "recommended" CVs are usually looked at first. Chileans use *pitutos* to speed up procedures, to get introduced to a company, or to gain favorable contractual terms. Although Chileans admire professionalism and knowledge, a *buen pituto* (a good connection) can often provide an employee with extra protection and speed up his or her career.

Chaqueteo is another interesting phenomenon that affects company life. *Chaqueteo* refers to the act of pulling someone by the jacket (of a man's suit) and describes the mischievous tendency of workmates to criticize and gossip about the work and commitment of more successful colleagues, in order to undermine their position and eventually ruin their reputation. This practice— which may have originated as a way to remove a "well-connected" colleague from his post—is also described as *aserruchar el piso*, literally, to saw the ground from under someone's feet. It is definitely not approved of. Today such practices are slowly disappearing, as companies try to achieve meritocracy through modern management techniques. As the legal framework becomes more stringent, and the general level of education improves, Chilean companies are becoming less hierarchical and traditional practices like *pituteo* and *chaqueteo* are gradually disappearing.

DOING BUSINESS WITH CHILEANS

Chileans are reserved; although they are friendly, they are not particularly open. In a business context they are less exuberant and laid back than Brazilians or Colombians. It is unlikely that your business contacts will take you out dancing, nor will they behave as if you were their best friend. You will almost certainly be invited for dinner and treated as a special guest, but, at least initially, the relationship will be more formal and you should be on your best behavior. Be relaxed and friendly, but remain professional. In personal relationships and in business, Chileans initially give very little away. They are diplomatic, generally correct, socially assured, but always careful about not revealing too much or creating conflicts.

To impress a Chilean business partner, be professional and punctual, avoid using an aggressive tone or a pushy negotiation style, and be patient. Avoid going straight to the point and talking business. Investing time and effort to build a relationship will prove invaluable—at the very least you should open a meeting or a business conversation with some small talk or general conversation. Chileans tend to make decisions slowly and prefer to avoid confrontation.

ARRANGING MEETINGS

Meetings can usually be organized by e-mail, although, when dealing with smaller companies, a phone call is generally more effective—particularly if you haven't received a reply to an e-mail! No reply is often equivalent to a "no." As many Chileans feel uncomfortable when refusing a request, they prefer to avoid giving a response altogether rather than openly rejecting a proposal. For these reasons Chileans are less likely to say "no" over the phone.

PUNCTUALITY AND FORMALITIES

Chileans themselves are divided over the matter of punctuality. They criticize their own inefficiency and the daily struggle to cope with delays, waiting times, and disorganization. Meetings frequently start later than expected: people may promise to be on time, but then reschedule at the last minute or keep you waiting endlessly. On the other hand, there are those who insist that meetings start on time, and they often do. A ten-minute delay is acceptable, but if you are going to be later than that, you should always call. Despite mixed practices, Chileans appreciate punctuality in business. To look professional, arrive on time.

Meetings always start with introductions and the exchange of business cards. Men shake hands; women kiss each other on the cheek. On introduction a man would normally kiss a woman on the cheek, unless she is much older or more senior. Spanish uses two forms of address, the formal *usted* and the informal *tú*. Start by using *usted* and only switch to *tú* if you notice that every Chilean at the meeting is doing so. Always address older or more senior counterparts as *usted*, unless they invite you specifically to use *tú*. People are addressed as *Señor* or *Señora* followed by their surname in the case of *usted*, or by the first name if addressed as *tú*.

Chileans prefer to bond before talking business. After introductions, people usually try to break the ice with some small talk. As a foreign guest, you might be asked questions about your country, your journey to Chile, or your initial impressions. The group sometimes discusses more general subjects such as sports or current affairs. If you are a Spanish speaker, don't be disoriented by the jokes, which are designed to put everybody at their ease.

As we have seen, the conduct of meetings depends on the sector, level of seniority and age of your counterparts, and geographical area. In sectors with international exposure, such as mining or finance, with younger foreign educated professionals, especially in Santiago, the style will be like that of Europe or the U.S.A. Discussions will probably be in English and the meetings are likely to be structured and focused. In sectors with limited or no international exposure, and with older or less senior counterparts, meetings with foreigners are often held in Spanish, sometimes with an interpreter.

At times, especially with smaller or provincial firms, you might also encounter a certain level of improvisation. Your Chilean counterparts might have forgotten to carry out agreed pre-meeting preparation work, such as organizing a projector or collecting the information you requested. You might have the feeling that they are promising more than they can deliver. Improvisation is often dictated by the desire to please and the reluctance to say "no." To avoid later disappointments and delays, discuss your requirements in advance and ask to see evidence of the services offered. Remember that Chileans are very respectful of written contracts, but feel less committed to verbal agreements. Always confirm commitments in writing and try to clarify as much as you can in person, as face-to-face discussions are much more effective than e-mails or phone calls.

NEGOTIATIONS AND DECISION MAKING

Chileans are nonconfrontational and disapprove of aggressive business tactics. Their style is reserved and they reveal little about their expectations and decisions. Negotiations should be carried out in a calm and diplomatic way, giving both sides the impression that they are free to decide in their own time. Do not expect a decision to be made during a meeting, and arm yourself with patience. Depending on the stage of the negotiations, meetings are a way to make an initial contact, gather information, and take the discussions further.

Decisions are made mostly at the highest level. As a Chilean manager puts it, companies make "personal" rather than team decisions. It is not unusual for internationally experienced but relatively junior staff to lead meetings with foreigners. It is not they who will decide. Decisions will ultimately be made after the meeting, and often through a long process, by their boss.

Negotiations over price are commonly accepted, but must be carried out in a subtle and professional way. Companies tend to specify discount rates in their price lists, but it is not unusual to negotiate further discounts or amend the standard terms. If you are selling to Chilean companies, be aware that they may ask at least three suppliers to produce estimates, or for large contracts may specify a formal tender process— which is likely to slow the sales cycle significantly.

ON NOT SAYING "NO"

As we have seen, Chileans are extremely averse to
conflict and do not like to say "no" openly. This can
be helpful during tough negotiations, as it will keep
the discussion civil. On the other hand, it can lead
to misunderstandings. For example, if Chileans do
not like your proposal, they will rarely
communicate a clear "no," but rather let the
relationship drift indefinitely, until you desist. Even
during preliminary discussions, Chileans rarely
express any dissatisfaction or negative comments,
and you may walk away from a meeting with a
positive impression, while in reality your contacts
are not interested. To achieve clarity, ask probing
questions and gently try to force your counterparts
to be more explicit. Ultimately, the most effective
way to break "Chilean diplomacy" is to foster your
relationship with the key decision makers outside
the office. Golf, dinners, or other social activities
will eventually increase the level of confidence and
trust that Chileans need in order to open up.

CONTRACTS

Chileans honor contracts. When purchasing
services, they generally accept contracts governed
by the law of the country in which the service
originates. For more complex agreements, check
with the Chamber of Commerce and, if necessary,

involve a legal expert. Chileans are very legalistic and take a long time to check a contract. They normally sign each page and expect to be able to change terms and conditions. Despite their legalism, they are practical and open to modern practices: electronic contracts are widely accepted, as are scanned copies of signed agreements.

BUSINESS ENTERTAINMENT

The Chileans like to "pamper" their foreign guests with invitations to delicious meals, and sometimes treats such as a weekend visit to the country. Breakfast meetings are purely a working session, with coffee and other refreshments. Business lunches are rather more relaxed. They can last several hours and you should keep the afternoon free, just in case. Wine is served, but should be drunk in moderation. Dinners can take place in restaurants or, if you have an established relationship, at home. Top businesspeople also like to organize dinner parties or meet at their private golf club. Established partners might even be invited for a weekend on the coast or in the mountains. (See Chapter 4 for tips on conversation topics and gifts.) Chilean hosts pay for everything and obviously expect similar treatment when they are abroad on business. Do not refuse invitations, as this might cause offense.

DRESS CODE

The dress code is generally formal. If you take Santiago's subway during the rush hour or go for a stroll in the main business areas, Santiago Centro and Las Condes, you will notice most men are in gray or dark blue suits with a briefcase and dark shoes.

Women wear formal pantsuits or sober dresses. They avoid bright colors and wear little makeup. In summer, women may wear sandals and lighter dresses, while men dress in pale colors, like beige or white. The dress code in NGOs and the media is often casual.

WOMEN IN BUSINESS

The Chilean attitude toward women is gradually changing. The number of women in key positions is growing, particularly in sales, business development, and marketing. Still, they are generally confined to middle management, and the top positions continue to be held by men. Foreign businesswomen will generally be well received. Chilean businessmen might behave flirtatiously at times, or appear overly courteous; however, women should accept this behavior as a sign of respect and hospitality. At the same time, senior foreign businesswomen might encounter some resistance from Chilean male counterparts, who may struggle to accept a woman's authority. This is particularly true in male-dominated sectors such as mining. Women should remember that a "power woman" approach is generally less effective than one that is firm, but nonaggressive.

Appropriate Behavior

A London businessman went to Santiago to meet a Chilean client and sign a contract for the sale of new equipment. After the first meeting, he invited his client to join him for a night out. The Chilean at first declined, but as the Englishman was insistent he accepted the offer. They went to a bar, where they had several rounds of drinks. The following day, the businessman was surprised by the Chilean's rather cold welcome and his reluctance to sign up to an additional order. The night out had not helped to foster their relationship—on the contrary, it had tarnished the Englishman's image as professional and reliable. First, he should have allowed the Chilean to make the overture. Then, Chileans do not drink for business entertainment. Had he invited his client for a quiet dinner, or better still, had he waited to be invited home, the business relationship would have developed further.

chapter nine

COMMUNICATING

CHILEAN SPANISH AND *CHILENISMOS*

Spanish, or *Castellano* as it is usually called in Latin America, is the official language of Chile. Indigenous languages are still spoken in a few communities, mainly by the older generations. The most important are Mapudungun (the Mapuche language) and Rapa Nui (the language of Easter Island). Many other native languages have died out. In the Lake Region a few German immigrants still speak German and read local publications in their language.

English is taught at school, but it is not widely spoken. In large towns and tourist centers it is relatively easy to get by without Spanish, but contact with locals will be limited. The situation is changing now that more Chileans are learning English and traveling abroad. In provincial towns it is not unusual to be stopped by children who are eager to practice their English. Still, Spanish is essential if you want to appreciate the country and the people.

Even if you are a beginner, don't be afraid as Chileans are normally patient with foreigners who try to speak their language. With Chilean Spanish, however, the problem will be to understand, rather than to speak.

To outsiders, Chilean Spanish can sound odd, difficult, and sometimes be incomprehensible. Chileans are, of course, aware of this, and are proud of their unique variant. They speak extremely quickly, shorten words by dropping consonants in the middle of the word as well as endings, and tend to use many colloquialisms that are obscure even to a native speaker from another Spanish-speaking country. There are no strong regional differences, but the language varies according to social class and level of education, although the most incomprehensible of all are young *santiaguinos*. The uniqueness of Chilean Spanish derives mainly from the thousands of *chilenismos* (typical Chilean expressions) that are used by people of all ages. *Chilenismos* are intriguing as they provide a fascinating insight into the culture.

If in doubt, always ask the meaning of an expression and don't use it unless you are really comfortable with it. Remember that some *chilenismos* are very rude, while others are neutral but can be extremely offensive in certain contexts. (See Further Reading for a good guide to the subject.)

SOME CHILENISMOS

Buscarle la quinta pata al gato (literally, to look for the fifth leg of the cat) means to make things overly complicated and more complex than they really are or to find imperfections or reasons for dissatisfaction with something.

Cachai (meaning "Do you understand?") is the most frequently used slang expression. It is also used as a form of feedback in conversation and comes from "Do you catch it?"

There are other hybrid forms of Chilenized and pure English expressions such as "*Cachala never*," referring to someone who never understands a joke!

Creerse la muerte (literally, to believe oneself to be death) means to consider oneself the best/the coolest. So an area of a famous beach resort where the upper-class Chilean youth gathers is known as El Cementerio (the cemetery)!

Arreglarse los bigotes (literally, to arrange one's mustache) refers to being successful in a love affair or fixing things cleverly to achieve the maximum advantage, for example in a business deal.

Like many other Latin Americans, Chileans use diminutives to indicate affection or intimacy, never the actual size. *Café* becomes *cafecito* and *pan, pancito*. The diminutive *chiquillos* (small children) can be used to address adults in a humorous way. Nicknames are also frequent and they normally refer to a person's characteristic (*el gordito*, the fat one) or are a short form of his/her name (*Pato* for *Patricio*).

Learning Spanish

Santiago has a wide variety of Spanish courses, but you can also find interesting options in the largest regional capitals and in tourist centers like Pucón and Punta Arenas. Course information is available on the Internet.

GREETINGS AND FORMS OF ADDRESS

Greetings follow a very precise protocol. Two women, or a woman meeting a man, kiss each other on the right cheek. Unlike many Europeans, Chileans only kiss once. Men shake hands. Good friends or relatives give each other a hug or a pat on the shoulder. This greeting is used in both formal and informal situations. In business or very formal meetings, a man should always gauge the age and level in the hierarchy of a woman, and opt for a handshake if she is older or more senior.

Despite the recent changes, Chile is still a traditional society where formalities play an important role. It is important to understand the rules governing the usage of the two Spanish forms of address, *tú* (informal "you") and *usted* (formal "you"), in order to avoid causing offense.

Usted is always used when the person addressed is older or more senior. This can result in "asymmetries," with the older person using *tú* and the younger *usted*. Nannies, for example, often address their employer as *usted*, but might be called *tú* in return. *Usted* is normally used between people who are not acquainted: in shops, offices, and so on. The transition from *usted* to *tú* is usually initiated by one of the parties (often the older or more senior) and marks the beginning of a closer relationship.

You may use *tú* with young people and in "trendy" environments. Among your peers, follow the Chileans' behavior and use *tú* only if they do. The same applies to business meetings, where *tú* is increasingly common, especially in the media or nonprofit sectors. Initially follow the Chileans; with time, you will develop an understanding of which form is most appropriate.

The term *Don* or *Doña* is used before the first name to indicate seniority and respect. It might be used by a secretary to refer to or address her boss, or by the nanny with her employers. It is quite old-fashioned and less used in more modern companies, but Chileans will always use it if they refer to someone by their first name and want to highlight distance and respect.

THE MEDIA
The Press

The Chilean press is controlled by two large groups, *Consorcio Periodístico* (*Copesa*) and *Empresa El Mercurio,* founded by the Edwards family in 1890. The two groups own a range of national and local newspapers. The Chilean press was very active prior to the 1973 coup, but was heavily controlled during the Pinochet dictatorship. Many newspapers closed or were forced to follow the government's guidelines. Even after the end of the dictatorship, Chilean press law remained restrictive and anachronistic: the freedom of the press was limited by a law that prosecuted any form of "offense to authority," making criticism very risky. In 1999 a journalist had to seek temporary exile to escape prosecution for libel following the publication of a book on the Chilean justice system. Today, a new press law is trying to eliminate such restrictions, which have been heavily criticized both in Chile and abroad.

El Mercurio is by far the most influential newspaper and the best in terms of international coverage (generally very limited), special reports, and weekend editions. It is the oldest daily and was the official newspaper under Pinochet, but it is now a prestigious conservative newspaper with high-quality articles. *La Tercera* is a more populist conservative newspaper and competes for readership with *El Mercurio*. There are many other dailies like *La Segunda* and *Las Últimas Noticias. La Quarta* is a sensationalist tabloid. *Estrategia* and *Revista Gestión* are the main financial newspapers, and *La Nación* is a government daily. Both regional and national dailies tend to have a so-called *Vida Social* (society) page, a showcase of high society, media VIPs, and, more rarely, charitable individuals.

The main weekly magazines are the conservative *Ercilla*, for politics and current affairs, and *El Punto Final*, a left-wing publication that was forced to close after the coup but reopened in 1989. *The Clinic* (named after the London hospital where Pinochet was arrested in 1998) is a fortnightly center-left satirical publication. There are plenty of glossy magazines, including the lifestyle magazine *Caras* and the Chilean version of *Hello!* magazine, *Cosas*.

Newspapers are sold at kiosks on the street, which in Santiago have a wide selection of foreign publications.

Television

Chile has six main TV channels. Many Chileans express dissatisfaction with the quality of the programing. News and quality information tend to be very limited, while TV shows and soap operas (*telenovelas*) predominate, although on some channels more than others. The main TV stations are the state-run Canal 7 TVN, with its international branch ChileTV, and the rival right-of-center Canal 13. Megavisión is a conservative private channel that broadcasts mainly soap operas and shows. Canal 11 Chilevisión is probably the most liberal of all, and Canal 5 UCV is a commercial TV channel that belongs to one of Chile's most prestigious private universities.

Cable TV was introduced in 1987 and has a wide variety of channels, including Latin American and non-Latin broadcasters like the BBC, CNN, and other foreign channels.

Radio

The radio is by far the most popular media in Chile. With more than 20 million radios and over 1,000 radio stations, radio reaches the most isolated areas of the country and the poorest groups. The most important stations are the state-run and omnipresent Radio Nacional de Chile and Radio Cooperativa, an informative service that vigorously opposed the dictatorship. Radio

Universidad de Santiago broadcasts both BBC News and Voice of America News.

MAIL

The Chilean postal service (Correos de Chile) is efficient and reliable. An air mail letter to Europe can take around four days. Post offices are open from 9:00 a.m. to 6:00 p.m. on weekdays and until 1:00 p.m. on Saturday. Postmen normally expect a tip for each letter they deliver, which is usually paid at the end of the month. Parcels must be collected at the post office.

TELEPHONES

Entel and Telefónica de Chile are the main phone operators. The many public pay phones are generally in good working order. Most use a prepaid card (*tarjeta telefónica*), on sale in stores. Annoyingly, many cards only work on telephones run by that particular operator. It is easier to go to a *centro de llamadas* (call center); these are found in all town centers and at some subway stations. The outgoing international code is 00, followed by the country code; national numbers are preceded by a local code that is omitted when you phone from the area itself. Calls are cheaper between 6:00 p.m. and 5:00 a.m. and on the weekend.

Cell phones are widely used. If you have a foreign cell phone, the cheapest option is to purchase a prepaid SIM card (*chip*) to avoid high roaming charges.

USEFUL NUMBERS

Chile does not have a central emergency number. Local operators are unlikely to speak English.

Police	133
Medical emergency	131
Fire department	132

INTERNET

Internet cafés (*centro internet* or *ciber café*) are available everywhere except in the smallest centers. They are often open until midnight and offer a wide range of services, including copying digital photos onto CDs and Internet calls. Internet centers cater to the majority of Chileans, who cannot afford a computer. According to a study by Spanish-owned Telefónica de Chile, the country has the highest number of Internet users in Latin America (still low at 27 percent, against 74 percent in the U.S.A.). Most users, however, are upper- or middle-class *santiaguinos*. The average price of a PC is higher than the average monthly income of 50 percent of the Chilean population.

CONCLUSION

We have seen that the Chileans' reserve sets them apart from the exuberant Latinos of other Latin American countries. Once trust is built, however, they welcome the stranger with warmth and generosity. Their fascination with anything foreign, coupled with their strong national pride, makes them attentive hosts. At first they will tend to extol the beauties of Chile and their national dishes; only later will they turn their attention to the foreign guest, making curious but always discreet inquiries about his or her country.

With time, though, this interest might wane, and the visitor will need to come to terms with a rather conservative society, where people rarely seek new contacts outside their family and their traditional circle of friends. Patience and flexibility are the keys to being accepted by Chileans, who can become extremely helpful, caring, and supportive friends.

The Chileans are an intriguing "mix" of Latino and European traits: the Spanish *conquistadores* clashed violently with the indigenous population, yet their cultures became intimately entwined, and were in turn shaped by the subsequent waves of European immigration. The Chileans' sense of hospitality and their relaxed attitude toward punctuality are typically

Latino. Similarly, they have a strong respect for hierarchies and center their life around the family and a close network of friends. In this conservative society, with its strong sense of class, personal connections and the right family background are the keys to success. These traditional values are now being questioned by the younger generation, and contrast with the efficiency, flexibility, and openness of modern Chilean society.

This is a particularly interesting moment in Chile's history. It is a country in transition, a traumatized nation that is still coming to terms with the abuse and repression of the Pinochet era, but also a stable democracy that is able to sustain a mature political debate, and that has just elected a woman president. Although many Chileans are still very traditional, this is slowly changing. In fact, the country's position as the Latin American stronghold of Catholicism is being challenged today by Chileans of all generations; pressure has recently led to unprecedented changes in family and censorship law.

Chile has the most stable economy in Latin America and is a strong economic player that exports a variety of key resources to the U.S.A, Europe, and Asia. The Chilean state controls the world's largest copper reserves. Nationalization, though, is the exception rather than the rule, in a country where foreign investors control some of the most important revenue-generating industries, such as telecommunications, fishing, and timber.

All these factors combine to make Chile an exciting place to visit. Above all, you cannot fail to admire the people whom you meet—for their warmth and dignity, their determination to succeed, their belief in transparency, democracy, and progress; and for their courage in questioning the past and fighting for justice.

Further Reading

Allende, Isabel. *My Invented Country: A Memoir*. London: Harper Perennial, 2004.

Beech, Charlotte, Jean-Bernard Carillet and Thomas Kohnstamm. *Lonely Planet: Chile and Easter Island*. London: Lonely Planet, 2006.

Brennan, John, and Alvaro Taboada. *How to Survive in the Chilean Jungle: An English Lexicon of Chilean Slang & Spanish Sayings*. Santiago: J.C. Sáez Editor, 2005.

Coloane, Francisco. *Cape Horn and Other Stories from the End of the World*. Pittsburgh: Latin American Literary Review Press, 2003.

García Márquez, Gabriel. *Clandestine in Chile: Adventures of Miguel Littín*. New York: Henry Holt, 1988.

Graham, Melissa. *The Rough Guide to Chile*. London: Rough Guides, 2003.

Muñoz, Luís. *Being Luís: A Chilean Life*. University of Exeter: Impress Books, 2005.

Wheeler, Sara. *Travels in a Thin Country: A Journey through Chile*. London: Abacus, 2004.

Williamson, Edwin. *The Penguin History of Latin America*. London: Penguin Books, 1992.

In-Flight Spanish. New York: Living Language, 2001.

Spanish. A Complete Course. New York: Living Language, 2005.

Fodor's Spanish for Travelers (CD Package). New York: Living Language, 2005.

culture smart! chile

Index

Acknowledgments

The author has drawn on many works in Spanish, including publications by Eugenio Tironi, Jorge Larraín, and Carlos Huneeus. Special thanks go to Lisette Gálvez for her invaluable contributions and friendship, and to Roberto Pagani for his support and insightful comments. Thanks also to Carmen Gloria Fuentealba from the Santiago Chamber of Commerce, Ricardo Pino and Andrés Medina, Annabelle Caballero, Cristian Álamos, and Jennifer Herbst.